T0306577

In the Mood for
CHEONGSAM

In the Mood for CHEONGSAM

TEXT BY
Lee Chor Lin AND
Chung May Khuen

EDITIONS DIDIER MILLET

N M
S
National Museum
of Singapore

Editorial Director: Douglas Amrine
Editor: James Lui
Designer: Louise Brody
Production Manager: Sin Kam Cheong

Published by
Editions Didier Millet Pte Ltd
121 Telok Ayer Street, #03-01
Singapore 068590
www.edmbooks.com
and

National Museum of Singapore
93 Stamford Road
Singapore 178897
www.nationalmuseum.sg

Colour separation by SC Graphic, Singapore

Printed by Tien Wah Press, Singapore

ISBN: 978-981-4260-92-3

Contents

Preface 9

Introduction
by Lee Chor Lin 13

The Evolving Meaning of the
Cheongsam from the 1950s to 1970s 35

Prominent Women 79

The Producers of Cheongsam 113

Glossary 147

Endnotes 152

Bibliography and Further Reading 156

Index 158

Picture Credits 159

Acknowledgements 160

PREFACE

Opposite: Photograph of a couple, 1940s. While the man was dressed in a Western suit, the woman was in a mid-calf length printed *cheongsam*.

This book is an effort to record the changing psyche and social landscape of a part of Singapore that has often escaped the attention of mainstream historians. Through the National Museum's collection of *cheongsam*, augmented in recent years, we are able to discern the underlying context in which Chinese women rose in public profile in Singapore society – first as prominent spouses and, after the Second World War, as a major source of labour, in both blue- and white-collar capacities.

It is interesting to find Chinese women in Singapore of different cultural and linguistic backgrounds embracing the *cheongsam* – the feminised form of the full-length Manchu male outfit – instead of the European suit as their dress code to represent modernity and a new self-awareness. In hindsight, we realise too that Singapore's unique historical circumstances allowed the *cheongsam* a relatively uninterrupted pace of evolution, as the dress was banned in Japanese-occupied Taiwan during the 1930s, and between the 1950s and 1989 it was shunned by women in mainland China.

We hope that readers will find in this book more than simply sartorial insights of Singapore society, for the golden age of *cheongsam* in Singapore is also intertwined with the intensive building of Singapore into a new nation.

We also take this opportunity to thank the Chinese Women's Association and its current President, Mrs Betty Chen, for taking a great interest in this project. Similarly, we are deeply grateful to all the donors who have kindly added their *cheongsam* to the Museum's collection.

Lee Chor Lin
Director
National Museum of Singapore

INTRODUCTION

Introduction[1]

by Lee Chor Lin

By the time China's two-millennium-old imperial ruling system was over-thrown in 1911, much of the urban population had already been through seven decades of exposure to an outside world dominated by European ascension, as well as a process of self-awakening, reform and drastic changes. Political transformation aside, writers and intellectuals from the traditional Chinese literati now embraced modern and liberal ideas. Young Chinese who were now populating universities in the great cities – Beijing, Tianjin, Nanjing, Shanghai – were poised to set trends for many aspects of the republican era.

More women enrolled in modern schools and universities which were based on American and European models. It had hitherto been unprecedented for women's voices to be heard widely, not only at elegant social gatherings but also on campuses, where women now took on roles on a par with their male counter-parts. To empower their newfound active and public role in society, there was a conscious push for women to update their public image. The old and brutal prac-tice of foot binding was condemned and abandoned by many; simple-cut blouses with narrower sleeves, worn with shorter skirts, were adopted with European leather shoes supported by strong heels; and hair was trimmed or bobbed.

On 4 May 1919, when a group of female Peking University students took to the streets with their fellow male students, they wore not the blouse-and-skirt ensemble that had been in vogue since the eve of the 1911 Revolution, but a version of the man's long robe (*changshan*), which was based on the now defunct Manchu *magua*. This female interpretation of *changshan* also eliminated the need for the trousers underneath, which the women substituted with full-length

Opposite: Studio portrait of a couple. While the man was dressed in Western garb, the woman wore a loose-cut *cheongsam* with wide sleeves and matched it with white stockings and T-bar shoes, late 1920s.

Page 10: Studio portrait of a *Peranakan* woman dressed in a *baju Shanghai*, c. 1910.

Page 11: Woman dressed in an ankle-length silk *cheongsam* on her wedding day.

stockings. As the enthusiasm and strength of the May Fourth Movement caught on in other major cities, particularly in Shanghai, *changshan* was wholeheartedly embraced not only by the ladies of Shanghai's high society, but by socialites, celebrities and prostitutes alike. This student look gave Chinese women the progressive and intellectual edge they had been looking for, as the Movement marked the watershed for an era of new hopes and aspirations.

In the following decades, Shanghai was to emerge as the voice of modernity for the Chinese world. There were critical factors that also contributed to the importance of Shanghai as such a centre: the speed of steamships that shortened the length of mail delivery and travel, the laying of deep-sea telephonic cables that made communication more immediately effective, the proliferation of newspapers and magazines, and the invention of cinema. The ascendance of the now republican and modern China would impact in many ways on the highly varied Chinese communities in Singapore and worldwide. For the Chinese people in Singapore, Shanghai was the beacon of all things new and fashionable. Much as the women here looked to style guides generated in London or Paris, the impact from Shanghai was more accessible and palpable.

Singapore during the second decade of the 20th century was a burgeoning city of prosperity and progress. A considerable portion of its wealth had been amassed locally in the hands of Chinese businessmen, who had by then become masters in their own right in the international entrepôt trade. This community of business-based interests was culturally diverse, for it included those Chinese *towkay* who had sprouted new wealth from scratch, as well as

TOP LEFT: A Chinese advertisement poster for cosmetics featuring a woman dressed in an ankle-length *cheongsam* with a very high collar typical of the 1930s.

MIDDLE: Studio portrait of a Chinese woman in *cheongsam*, 1930s. She sported a short hair-do and a slim *cheongsam*, which was in fashion then as compared to the looser *cheongsam* of the late 1920s.

TOP RIGHT: A Chinese advertisement poster from a tobacco company. Taking centre stage is a woman dressed in a stylish 1920s floral *cheongsam* with bell sleeves.

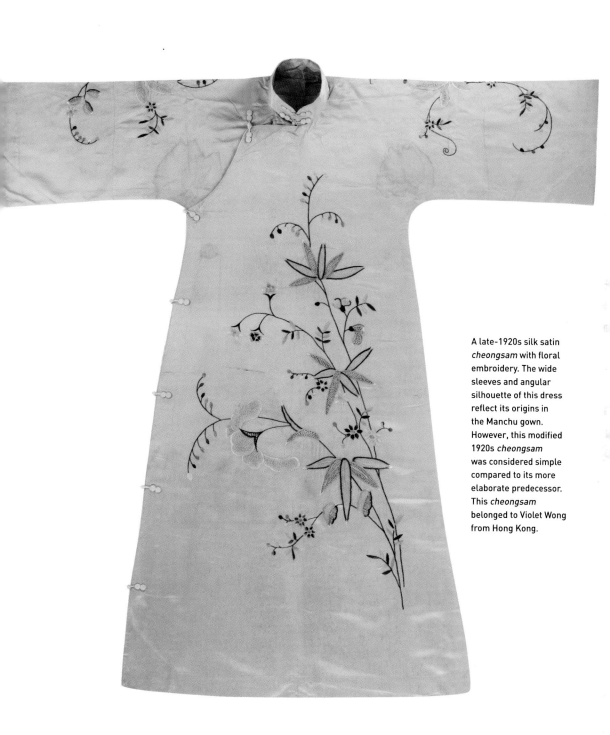

A late-1920s silk satin *cheongsam* with floral embroidery. The wide sleeves and angular silhouette of this dress reflect its origins in the Manchu gown. However, this modified 1920s *cheongsam* was considered simple compared to its more elaborate predecessor. This *cheongsam* belonged to Violet Wong from Hong Kong.

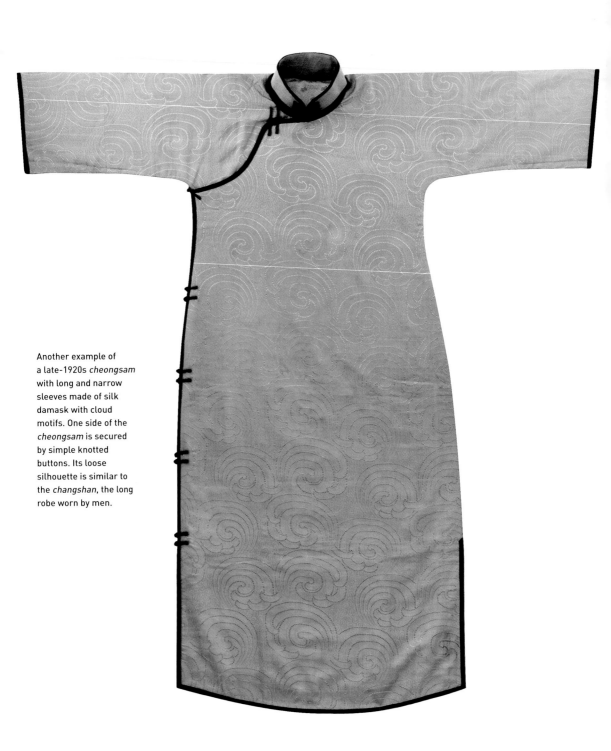

Another example of a late-1920s *cheongsam* with long and narrow sleeves made of silk damask with cloud motifs. One side of the *cheongsam* is secured by simple knotted buttons. Its loose silhouette is similar to the *changshan*, the long robe worn by men.

the worldly Straits-born *Peranakan* men (*baba*s) of older establishments with lucrative East-West business connections. Whether by way of modern China or the British, the Singapore business circle understood that knowledge and education were key to the sustainability of their wealth, and their bargaining chip with the colonial masters. As early as late 19th century, they had embarked on school projects to provide the teaching of modern tools of survival as well as the Chinese language for the larger milieu of male children, as well as girls.

This was also a time when a large influx of female immigrants appeared in Singapore for reasons ranging from job prospects to marriage. As the female population within the Chinese community increased visibly, dress style became a more urgent identifier, as many Chinese women were living in close proximity to those from other dialect groups, different social backgrounds, and, increasingly, of various educational levels. Previously, Chinese women would hardly have left their households, let alone have travelled to other districts even within their own provinces. Now in Singapore, local customs and ways of doing things back home suddenly became very important so that women could differentiate themselves from the Cantonese or the Hainanese, for example. Hence for a segment of Chinese women who remained domestic, the robe-and-baggy-trousers ensemble was still a staple dress form. The idea of wearing men's *changshan* without the trousers would be, to them, as scandalous as it would be radical.

However, for those women who left domesticity behind to embrace the brave new world through education and social exposure, the choice of clothes was no longer purely an individual one but also one that was guided by their peers and society. There was a need to identify oneself with progress and modern ways. One of the most direct and obvious methods was by changing one's

outlook and switching to wearing clothes that were consistent with popular trends. Some Straits-born or *Peranakan* women (*nonya*s) were keenly attuned to the rapidly changing sartorial trends in Europe and China. Despite a tropicalised Southeast Asian lifestyle and a daily persona in *sarong kebaya*, the traditional *nonya*s had to wear elaborate costumes in southern Chinese style on formal occasions, most notably during their wedding ceremonies. Since the 20th century, however, *Peranakan* brides or young women engaged to be married would appear in photo studios wearing what was called the *baju Shanghai*, the skirt-and-blouse ensemble popularly worn by fashionable Chinese women during the period after 1911 and in the early 1920s. The long-sleeved silk tunics were reminiscent of the *baju panjang* (long blouse), but the collars and the asymmetric fastening system, as well as the embroidery, suggest that they were made to special order by Chinese seamstresses and tailors. Often tailored from the same material as the tunic, the long skirts would be pleated but without the central panel at the front, as seen on wedding costumes. As the name suggested, they were most likely the work of the prolific tailors of Shanghainese or Cantonese origins who had by the first decade of the 20th century set up shop in Singapore. This ensemble of tunic and pleated skirt seemed widely popular amongst the young *Peranakan* women, as seen in family portraits of the time. The presence of their matriarch in *sarong kebaya*, and sometimes their unique hairdo, in these portraits characterise their *Peranakan* identity.

In wealthy *Peranakan* families, who enjoyed extensive interaction with the larger cosmopolitan community, the presence of siblings returning from studies in Europe or visiting business associates from abroad nurtured a tendency for the educated *nonya* to adopt an international, urban dress style, as she would

Top left and right: Studio portraits of two young girls in the *sam* (blouse) and *kun* (skirt) ensemble, 1920s. This outfit was worn by educated females and younger women, and co-existed with the *cheongsam* until the early 1930s.

Middle: Advertisement poster for Shandong Yuxing fabric dyes, showing the wide-sleeved jacket-blouse paired with calf-length trousers or skirt, a fashion that flourished following the May Fourth Movement.

Opposite: *Cheongsam* in lace with colourful floral embroidery, late 1930s to early 1940s. This sheer *cheongsam* would be worn with a slip underneath. The collar and the asymmetrical opening are decorated with floral fastenings while the side is secured with press studs.

LEFT: Portrait of a woman dressed in a *cheongsam* with large polka dot motifs, early 1940s.

OPPOSITE:
1. Studio portrait of a young woman dressed in a *cheongsam*, 1930s.

2. A group photograph of four young women on an excursion. While one was dressed in the *sarong kebaya*, the other three wore the slim-cut *cheongsam*, 1930s.

3. Rubber tycoon Lim Nee Noon and his *Peranakan* family at Marsiling Villa, 1934. While the matriarch (seated in the front row) was dressed in the traditional *sarong kebaya*, the younger women in the second and third rows wore the *cheongsam*.

4. Woman with permed hair dressed in a *cheongsam* and a Western cape, 1930s.

5. Portrait of a Chinese man with two women dressed in loose-cut ankle-length *cheongsam*, early 1940s.

occasionally play host to guests alongside her male family members. The *Peranakan* wife of tycoon Lee Choon Guan (1868–1924), Tan Teck Neo (1877–1978), who was herself daughter of *baba* tycoon and community leader Tan Keong Saik (whom Keong Saik Road was named after), for instance, was often seen, from the early 1920s onwards, in the cosmopolitan Chinese-style silk dress-and-blouse ensemble entertaining friends in her seaside villa, travelling, and hosting formal functions. Likewise, the wife of Song Ong Siang, another prominent *Peranakan* tycoon and author of *One Hundred Years' History of the Chinese in Singapore*, wore a splendid silk *changshan* with white stockings and European shoes to attend the 1926 opening of King Edward VII College of Medicine Building, but her hair remained coiffed in beautiful and neat *nonya* style. This was probably the moment when *changshan* had already become acknowledged as a formal dress in the Singapore scene, but known more by its Cantonese pronunciation, *cheongsam*, by way of Cantonese-speaking tailors and domestic help.

Therefore, as the *cheongsam* was seen by *nonya*s like Mrs Lee and Mrs Song in the 1930s as the trendy style for Chinese around the world, it increasingly replaced the *sarong kebaya* as the appropriate dress for formal occasions. They wore their *cheongsam* with diamond-studded *kerosang* brooches (normally used for fastening the *kebaya*) and impressive *Peranakan* jewellery. Certainly by the 1930s, *nonya*s in their twenties would wear *cheongsam* to pose for family portraits, sometimes with their hair styled in the latest permanent wave or cut short, leaving their mothers and older female relatives to persist in wearing *sarong kebaya*.

Those non-*Peranakan* Chinese women who came from families with strong connections to mainland China, and those who had been influenced by the contemporaneous values of modernity, would also look to Shanghai for inspiration, especially in fashion. By the 1920s, in addition to the female contingents of wealthy and prominent families, the Chinese female demography in Singapore included white-collar workers, who were mostly Chinese schoolteachers, and

1

2

3

4

5

wives of middle-class professionals who were themselves products of modern Chinese education. All these women found themselves increasingly appearing in public spaces: the affluent wives and daughters at dinner parties and social gatherings, and the teachers and white-collar workers at their workplaces, on public transport, and hence in the wider social milieu.

The need to appear in attire that was commensurate with their reformed cultural and social background was important. The Chinese-medium education they received allowed them direct access, through printed matter, magazines and advertising, to the latest sartorial developments in Shanghai and Hong Kong. Strong real-life models promoting the wearing of *cheongsam* sprung up as more women became actively engaged in public spheres. A new generation of female writers such as Eileen Chang (Zhang Ailing 张爱玲) engaged in regular healthy discourses on fashion and national identity in popular illustrated magazines such as *The Companion Pictorial* (*Liangyou* 良友). Emerging female intellectuals such as Lin Huiyin 林徽音 – whose Revolutionary martyr pedigree and privileged European education gave her access to the most exclusive circle of modern literati (such as Lu Xun 鲁迅 and Xu Zhimo 徐志摩), occasionally playing hostess to visiting laureates such as George Bernard Shaw and Rabindranath Tagore – typified her generation of highly educated women, especially with the custom-made *qipao* 旗袍, by which the *changshan* was now more widely known in Mandarin, meaning "Manchu gown". The beautiful and dynamic Soong Mei-ling 宋美龄, wife of Generalissimo Chiang Kai-shek 蒋介石, demonstrated the efficacy of woman power – visiting peasants and wooing the American public for China's causes in well-coordinated long stately versions of the dress. Equally trend-sensitive and with spending power, Chinese women in Singapore tailed Shanghai's whims and fancies with great expediency. The *cheongsam* or *qipao* (in the Mandarin milieu) was naturally the preferred

Black *cheongsam* in silk
satin with an abstract
motif of a sailing boat
and double piping, 1940s.
The sleeves are made
from a single piece of
fabric and the shoulders
are cut straight, both
features of *cheongsam*
from the 1930s to the
1940s. These features
made the dress from
this period restrictive
to the wearer. The collar
and the asymmetrical
opening are decorated
with flower buttons
and the side was secured
with press studs.

This see-through floral *cheongsam* with a burn-out pattern effect on velvet was popular amongst women in the 1930s. It has narrow short sleeves and a fitted waistline. It was worn with a slip underneath. The high collar was lined with a panel of lace on the inside. This lace lining could be replaced with a new one when it became dirty or stained. It carried the label of Yue Tai Cheong Silk Shop, one of the earliest tailor shops in Singapore to make *cheongsam* in the early 20th century.

OPPOSITE: Photograph of two seated women dressed in *cheongsam*, 1930s. The woman on the left was probably wearing a velvet floral *cheongsam* with a burn-out effect. Both of them were opera performers who came from China.

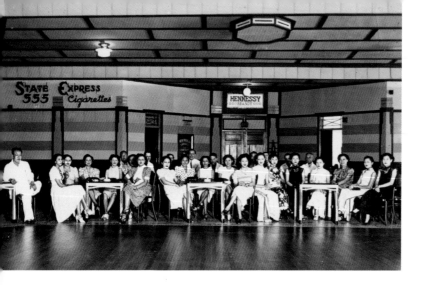

dress, which these women wore like a uniform, embellishing and accessorising them in line with European and American trends then.

The prevalence of Cantonese and Shanghainese tailors who set up shop in High Street, North Bridge Road and Bras Basah Road in the business district offered women a good range of top-class workmanship as well as ample choice in fabrics. Within each neighbourhood, smaller tailor shops with perhaps a smaller repertoire could satisfy the needs of women with lesser means.

It was clear that by the mid-1930s, Chinese women were more promi-nent in wider social contexts, as noticed by British colonial officer R. H. Bruce Lockhart who returned in 1933 for a visit after 25 years of absence: "Gone, too, is the former seclusion of the better-class Chinese women, and to-day Chinese girls, some bespectacled, some passingly beautiful, but all serious, all with bobbed and permanently waved hair in place of the former glossy straightness, and all dressed in semi-European fashion, walk vigorously through the streets on their way to their studies or to their games."[2] Graduation photographs of female-only classes also appeared with greater frequency in the 1930s. While some students sat for the pictures in their school uniform, many would be in *cheongsam*, which had obviously become the dress for women who had reached adulthood and had become a mark of significant personal achievements, such as the completion of one's education. That the dress had also transcended the language boundary between graduates of Chinese-medium schools and those of English schools to become a universally accepted code of dress for high-achieving for Chinese women was noticeable in a 1941 group photograph of the English-medium Raffles College's Historical & Economics Societies Combined Fancy Dress Social, in which the Chinese female cohorts were dressed largely in *cheongsam* or *qipao*, like many female Chinese elite elsewhere.

A salmon pink *cheongsam* made of silk crêpe with floral embroidery, 1930s. The *cheongsam* was worn with a slip that has scalloped edging. This dress was worn by a bride on her wedding day.

OPPOSITE: A group of *cheongsam* made of silk crêpe and velvet with floral motifs from the 1930s to early 1950s.

The Evolving Meaning of the *Cheongsam* from the 1950s to 1970s

The Evolving Meaning of the
Cheongsam from the 1950s to 1970s

The 1950s and 1960s were the golden period of the *cheongsam* as an everyday dress in Singapore. The traditional one-piece dress, which had an elitist image before the outbreak of the Second World War (1942–1945), was no longer just popular wear for the wives of wealthy businessmen, young girls from prominent Chinese families and teachers. Instead, it was appropriated by working women as a trendy form of daily wear. The choice of everyday dress is determined and influenced by fashion and by social factors, such as class, gender, ethnicity, age, occupation, income and body shape.[1] Thus, a study of the *cheongsam*'s development in Singapore after the war will have to take into account the major shift in identity of women from being traditional homemakers to modern working women as a result of the country's changing political, economic and social climate. The increased presence of women in public spaces after the war clearly had an impact on the symbolic meaning of the *cheongsam* and the wearing of it. The adaptability of the *cheongsam* to changes in fashion and, more importantly, the creativity of its consumers helped give the dress its status as an everyday dress associated with modernity during the post-war period.

The Power Shifts: Women in Politics

> ... the 1950s and 1960s were the era of action. These were the decades when increasing numbers of Singapore women earned a wage, when they obtained the vote and when they came to demand much more from the society to which they belonged.[2]

The emancipation of Singapore women, which was interrupted by the war, resumed at a great pace from the late 1940s onwards. Women began to participate in the country's politics in the context of rising nationalism and anti-colonialist sentiments. Between 1948 and 1951, four English-educated women – Mrs Robert Eu, Ms Amy Laycock, Mrs Vilasini Menon and Mrs Elizabeth Choy – lent their voices to the nation's politics.[3] Although they came from middle-class families and were elected by a predominately English-educated electorate, their presence in the City and Legislative Councils indicated the start of the political mobilisation of women after the war.

The 1950s were also characterised by the proliferation of women's organisations in Singapore, helmed by women. In 1952, one of the more important institutions, the Singapore Council of Women (SCW), was established by a group of women leaders to fight for equal rights for women and against polygamy; it had a membership of 2,000 women.[4] By 1955, women were recognised as a significant force by political parties when the proportion of women voters increased dramatically from 8 per cent to 50 per cent due to the automatic registration of all voters. In the Progressive Party and the Labour Party, "Women's Sections" were created. In 1956, the People's Action Party (PAP) Women's League was formed by Mdm Chan Choy Siong, Mdm Ho Puay Choo and Mdm Oh Siew Chen to fight for equal rights and opportunities as well as equal pay for women.[5] Mdm Chan was largely responsible for pushing women's issues to the forefront in the PAP.[6] In 1959, she and seven other women candidates were elected to the Legislative Assembly. The other prominent female representative and first woman in opposition was Mrs Seow Peck Leng.[7] Both Mdm Chan and Mrs Seow symbolised an increasingly active womanfolk who assumed leadership roles in areas that were previously dominated by males.

Top left: The presence of Mrs Elizabeth Choy (left) and Mrs Vilasini Menon (right) in the Legislative Council marked the increasing presence of women in politics, 1950.

Middle: Mrs Seow Peck Leng, the first female opposition member voted into the Legislative Assembly, attending the inaugural session of the Assembly, 1959.

Top right: A fashionably dressed woman in sunglasses and a polka dot sleeveless *cheongsam* being interviewed for her views about the elections, 1955.

Rayon sleeveless *cheongsam* with polka dots. *Cheongsam* for day wear were usually simple in design. Mdm Wu Chuen Chuen, the owner of Stamford Café (late 1940s to late 1960s), wore this simple but elegant *cheongsam* to work.

The passing of the Women's Charter Bill in 1961 by the PAP government further enhanced the social status of women. Polygamy was outlawed and matters related to marriage, divorce and property-ownership would be regulated (though not for Muslims). When the Bill was passed in the Legislative Assembly, Mdm Chan Choy Siong declared in Mandarin, "Although this Bill will not provide for equal pay among men and women, it will, however, make them fully realise their political, educational, cultural and economic equality in society."[8] A year later, the government instituted the principle of equal pay for equal work in the civil service.[9]

Women at Work

The rush to mobilise women into the economy was pursued vigorously by the government in the early 1960s. This was represented by the policy of rapid industrialisation that concentrated on labour-intensive, low-value industries such as textiles, which required little skill or capital layout.[10] In 1965, export-oriented industrialisation was introduced. In response to the government's call for economic development and progress for the nation, women's participation in the workforce increased by about 8 per cent, from 17.5 per cent in 1957 to 25.8 per cent in 1970.[11] Women also began to venture beyond traditional occupations, such as teaching and nursing, with 40 per cent of the female workforce employed in manufacturing industries, such as electronics and textile factories, and another 29 per cent in retail trade or in restaurants and hotels.[12]

Education policies introduced by the government during this period were also aligned with its call to involve women in the nation's economy. Funds were allocated to the building of schools and extra efforts were made to recruit and train teachers after the war. Universal free education for both boys and girls

Top left: Women casting their votes on Polling Day, 30 May 1959.

Middle: Elected member for the West, Mrs Robert Eu, addressing the crowd at the opening of the new infant and welfare clinic at Aljunied Road, 1956.

Top right: A group of female trainee teachers at the Teachers' Training College, 1950.

Orange silk *cheongsam* with floral motifs and a matching long-sleeved jacket. The jacket has a V-shaped neckline and is decorated with three horizontal panels at the waist.

was achieved by the time of independence in 1965. Hence women were being equipped with the basic skills which employers valued.

In 1957, attendance in English-medium schools had risen to four times the pre-war figure in 1941.[13] Most parents felt that an English education provided their children with better prospects for employment and for attaining a higher tertiary education. In 1960 the first integrated schools were opened where pupils could study in different languages but mingle socially under the same roof, and 84 such schools were built in the next seven years.[14] The greater importance given to English, multilingualism, scientific and technical studies, and to physical fitness training,[15] had an impact on the increasingly Westernised and cosmopolitan outlook of women and this was reflected in the way they wore the *cheongsam*.

Furthermore, the successful introduction of family-planning services in the 1950s and 1960s helped free women from their traditional reproductive role. This in turn allowed them to join the workforce and pursue other activities outside of home. In 1949, the Singapore Family Planning Association (SFPA) was established by Mrs Constance Goh Kok Kee and a group of female volunteers. Mothers were provided with contraceptive supplies, and information about family planning and birth-control methods was disseminated.[16] Although family planning was initially resisted due to religious and privacy reasons and a largely conservative population, by 1966, the campaigns' success was registered in the decline of the birth rate from 45 per thousand in 1949 to 30 per thousand.[17] The government also launched efforts such as "Stop at Two" and took over the official role of family planning in 1966.

Political emancipation, rapid economic development and social changes in Singapore provided the necessary impetus for the modernisation and Westernisation of women in the 1950s and 1960s. Opportunities to pursue an

education provided them access to a wider range of jobs while social changes such as the promotion of family planning and society's increasing acceptance of working women meant that they could now pursue a career and spend more time on leisure activities. There was also an increase in cultural inter-action amongst the different ethnic groups with the expansion of the role of women in society. In light of these changes, women felt an urgent need to dress appropriately outside of their homes and the *cheongsam* they wore could no longer be just an ethnic marker. Instead, it had to assume a greater role in signifying their new position in society.

The *Cheongsam* as a Symbol of Modernity

From the 1950s onwards, as women coped with their new public roles, they discovered the importance of the dress as a presentation of self, through which they expressed their individual identity and also came to be read by others. Joanne Entwistle has noted that dress is crucial as a presentation of self.[18] Before the 1950s, the *cheongsam* was a traditional Chinese dress worn by ladies from well-to-do families including the Straits-born Chinese. It was trendy and took its cue from the fashion capitals of Shanghai and Hong Kong. It was expensive because it was custom-made and hence affordable only to the wealthy and was worn on special occasions. It was also associated with Chinese teachers who came to Singapore to teach[19] even though the *cheongsam* they wore were much simpler. Although it continued to be a popular choice of dress for the elite after the Second World War, it was quickly adopted by working women in Singapore as a stylish everyday dress suitable for offices, schools and commercial firms.

義安女學校第二十屆畢業生攝影元旦年壬月芒日

LEFT: Group photo of a graduating class at Ngee Ann Girls' School, 1963. The teachers seated in front are dressed in simple *cheongsam*.

OPPOSITE: Polyester *cheongsam* with capped sleeves and Pucci-inspired prints, late 1960s; sleeveless jersey *cheongsam* with psychedelic motifs, 1970s; sleeveless silk georgette *cheongsam* with floral motifs and accompanying slip with lace trimmings, late 1960s; silk *cheongsam* with abstract floral motifs, late 1960s.

There are several reasons for this. First, the *cheongsam* of the post-war period retained the tight-fitting silhouette that was introduced and popularised by the "New Look".[20] While some women were quick to abandon the traditional *cheongsam* for tight-fitting Western frocks, there were others who chose to appropriate the necessary elements into the *cheongsam* that they felt would project them as modern and progressive as their new roles demanded. Dr Angela Partington of the School of Creative Arts, the University of the West of England, noted, "The consumer's investment in a style may or may not involve a transformation of the fashion commodity's appearance, but more like [a] reworking of the object. They are social acts in which the object only has meaning in relation to the circumstances surrounding them. Hence a 'reproductive transformation' takes place."[21] Indeed, the previously loose-fitting *cheongsam* in Singapore was now updated with a nipped-in waist which provided the desired modern air to the representation of ethnic identity for its wearer. Professor Joanne Finkelstein further argued that "society progress[es] from change, fashion is a form of change and fashion measures intellectual engagement as it reflects a society's level of civilisation and sensitivity toward achieving progress."[22] The adaptation of a Western silhouette in *cheongsam* which accentuated the figure of the wearer was significant as it corresponded with the changing identity of Singapore women living in an increasingly cosmopolitan society, exposed to Western ideas and fashion.

Singapore women as consumers of the *cheongsam* were not the only group that was inspired by the new look. Even tailors became aware that their customers preferred to wear dresses with a tight-fitting silhouette. Shanghainese tailors such as Master Lok Chye Kwai reflected that new techniques had to be introduced into the making of the *cheongsam* in response to the modernised form:

FAR LEFT: Many women in the 1960s wore a *cheongsam* and sported a beehive hairdo to work, such as Mrs Nancy Lim shown here at her office, 1965.

LEFT: Mrs Nancy Lim drove to work in a fitted *cheongsam* every day, 1960.

OPPOSITE:
1. The uniform of a female staff at the Product and Design Centre of the John Little Building was a long-sleeved *cheongsam*, 1965.

2. All female employees at Chung Khiaw Bank had to wear a *cheongsam* to work every day.

3. A model stepping out of a BOAC Comet during a fashion show at Robinsons in Singapore flanked by two BOAC air stewardesses from Hong Kong, 1959.

4. The majority of the factory workers at the Bata shoe factory at Telok Blangah were women, 1964.

5. Women were mobilised into the work force in the 1950s and 1960s as a result of the country's rapid industrialisation. A group of female sales representatives dressed in *cheongsam* and Western frocks at the cosmetics booth at Great World, 1961.

Darts were introduced in the 1950s and 1960s as the fashion then was for a more form-fitting silhouette. Cheongsam became more fitted and three dimensional to the upper part of the garment to make it look like a Western dress.[23]

Mrs Nancy Lim recounted the wasp-waist *cheongsam* as a popular dress for girls working in the office in the 1960s.[24] She wore the *cheongsam*, carried a briefcase and drove to work everyday. It was not only an image which, as she proudly declared, distinguished her from her colleagues who wore Western frocks but it also helped to leave a deep impression on her clients. She felt extremely confident and professional in her Westernised tight-fitting *cheongsam*. Similarly, Mrs Lau Siew Yee found the *cheongsam* more professional and elegant compared to the Western frocks and the *samfoo*.[25]

In Chung Khiaw Bank, a home-grown enterprise,[26] *cheongsam* was the designated uniform for all female employees. Ms Rosalind Leong related that female employees could wear the *cheongsam* in any colour they liked and even though she did not like wearing it, she admitted that "[i]t does give that distinguished look" and "I don't have to think of a pattern, or rack my head about what to wear to the office".[27] In 1963, Chung Khiaw Bank started a special "Lady in Pink" service whereby female staff dressed in pink *cheongsam* would attend to women customers in an attempt to make bank services popular among women.[28] The *cheongsam* was also popular as a uniform for other service industries. For example, Chinese flight attendants from the British Overseas Airways Corporation (BOAC, the precursor of British Airways) and Belgian airline SABENA wore the *cheongsam* as their uniform.

Another element that indicated the Westernisation of *cheongsam* was the wearing of Western-style jackets over the form-fitting garment. For women in the offices, the jacket provided a smart and businesslike look. It could also transform the sleeveless *cheongsam* into a dress suitable for formal functions. During the 1960s, the jacket became even more popular with the introduction

of air conditioning in numerous public spaces. The practice of updating the *cheongsam* extended to wearing it with a clutch bag, gloves, medium or high-heeled shoes and other accessories. Throughout the two decades from the 1950s, the hemline, sleeves and collar of the *cheongsam* changed in accordance with contemporary Western fashion, making it an enduring dress embraced by women in Singapore seeking to keep up with the times.

Celebrities, Fashion Magazines and Films as Cultural Producers

Before the advent of television in Singapore in 1963, many women found out about the latest fashion from the dress styles of popular actresses on the silver screen, especially Malay and Chinese movies produced by home-grown studios such as the Shaw Brothers and Cathay-Keris Film Productions which dominated Singapore's film industry from the mid-1930s to the 1960s. For example, when famous Chinese actresses Ge Lan (Grace Chang) and Lin Dai (Linda) wore stylish slim-fitting *cheongsam* with matching jackets in several of their films in the 1950s and 1960s, the look was enthusiastically taken up by women in Hong Kong and Singapore. Cultural intermediaries, such as popular local magazines *Saturday Review*[29] and *Her World*, film magazines such as *Screen Voice* and *Kong Ngee* as well as *The Straits Times* featured the latest Western fashions, updates on *cheongsam* and tips on dressing up.

The World of Synthetics and the Modern *Cheongsam*

In the 1950s, the development of the *cheongsam* as a chic garment in Singapore received a boost when the country overtook Bangkok as the regional distribution centre for textiles because of its entrepôt trade and free port status.[30] Textile trader Sachdev Durgadass explained, "At first, Bangkok was the centre

Top left: Malayan singer Eng Wah performing a number dressed in a tight-fitting silk satin black *cheongsam*, 1956.

Middle: Poster depicting popular Hong Kong actress Le Di (乐蒂) dressed in an extremely tight-fitting pink silk satin *cheongsam* decorated with embroidered motifs, early 1960s.

Top right: Models dressed in pencil-slim *cheongsam*, *sarong kebaya* and the Western frock showing off the latest shoe trends at the Bata fashion show in Singapore, 1963.

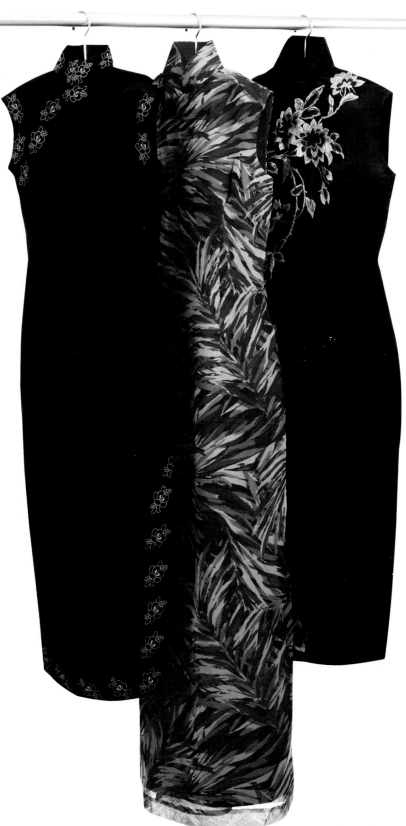

RIGHT: Fabrics with a shiny surface, such as silk satin, and ankle-length *cheongsam* were reserved for formal occasions. Black *cheongsam* with embellishments or embroidery were also well-liked by women in the 1950s and 1960s.

FOLLOWING PAGES: A group of floral, geometric, abstract and paisley printed *cheongsam*, 1950s to 1960s. Capped sleeves and sleeveless *cheongsam* were the desired style because of the tropical weather in Singapore.

TOP LEFT: Women who wanted to purchase European silks and laces would frequent shops along High Street, Singapore, 1965.

TOP RIGHT: Textile store in Chinatown, 1962.

OPPOSITE: Yellow *cheongsam* with capped sleeves in silk and decorated with shimmery silver trimming, late 1960s; green sleeveless *cheongsam* in Swiss cotton, 1960s; and blue laced *cheongsam* with capped sleeves embellished with cording and scalloped hem, late 1960s.

FOLLOWING PAGES: While men dressed up in tuxedos and bow ties, the *cheongsam* was the preferred formal wear for women attending banquets and wedding dinners, 1960s. Mdm Wu Chuen Chuen, the lady owner of Stamford Café, is seated on the extreme left.

for distribution for the Southeast Asia market. But after the war, Singapore was the centre. This was because of the financial institutions. You could easily open up LOC [Letters of Credit]. Ships were regularly plying and it was easier to do business here. You could ship goods anywhere."[31] This meant that women were able to purchase the trendiest fabrics for their *cheongsam* from Europe, America and Asia along High Street and Arab Street in Singapore. Women who needed affordable yet fashionable clothes for the office also enjoyed imported cheap synthetic fabrics from Japan and later Korea.

The introduction of man-made fibres in 1950s was timely because women needed a stylish yet practical wardrobe that catered to their various needs. Mr Jaswant Singh Bajaj, a textile merchant, aptly described the impact of synthetics on the working woman in the 1950s:

> Along with the introduction of the new synthetic textiles, people began to become conscious of what they were wearing. ... Women also began to become "more fashion conscious". There was more money to spend. As a result, textile traders had to become more innovative and could no longer stick to cottons but instead being [able] to store synthetics, nylons and materials in new designs. The working girl needed new clothing every week – something different and something new. 52 weeks meant 52 dresses per year.[32]

In the decade after the war, these artificial fabrics were popular because of the conveniences they offered to consumers. They were affordable, durable, lightweight and crease-resistant with easy-care qualities. For example, unlike the traditional silk ones, women did not have to dry-clean their synthetic *cheongsam* after each wear. Also, they did not have to worry about over-washing. In addition, dirt could easily be removed from synthetics.

Besides being valued for the conveniences they offered, synthetic fabrics were also popular for their designs in the 1960s. Synthetics raised consumer expectations for more variety in pattern and texture.[33] The wearing of brightly coloured clothes with floral, geometric, Optical Art illusion and psychedelic prints was not restricted to Westernised youths. *Cheongsam* made of polyester, jersey and lurex[34] printed with Pop Art motifs began to emerge as an important statement in the wardrobes of the young and stylish. Singapore's status as a textile hub meant that synthetic fabrics in all sorts of colours and designs from all over the world were easily available. Women who were adventurous and innovative began to appropriate these "raw materials", offered by the existing fashion industry of the 1960s, and to create a diversified and modern wardrobe that was different from those of their mothers and aunts. In this case, it was also about expressing their identity as modern working women with taste as they adjusted to their new role in society. Modernity opened up new possibilities for the creation of identity.[35]

A New Set of Aesthetics: Experimenting with Local Fabrics

According to Singaporean sociologist Chua Beng Huat, the culture of the daily lives of Singaporeans is the enduring result of the mixing, or hybridisation, of the cultures of people who came to Singapore in search of a living. From commercial transactions to chance encounters among strangers, interactions among Singaporeans involved extensive ethnic and linguistic code mixing.[36] Cultural interaction amongst various ethnic groups in Singapore was encouraged with the opening up of integrated schools and women entering the workforce. This form of interaction was manifested in the hybrid *cheongsam* of the post-war period.

Besides incorporating man-made fibres introduced by new technology in the making of the modern *cheongsam*, resourceful women began to experiment with fabrics that were commonly associated with other ethnic communities in Singapore. For example, both Mrs Nancy Lim and Mrs Lau Siew Yee recalled

OPPOSITE: A mosaic of trends – in the 1950s and 1960s, Singapore women took great pains to dress up so as to project a trendy modern image. This included doing their hair in bouffant styles and the wearing of wigs, gloves and other accessories usually associated with the West. A stylish way of supplementing one's *cheongsam* included adorning it with flowers, a brooch or a necklace. To further distinguish themselves from what other women wore, some of them used *batik* or Kelantan Silk to make *cheongsam*. The woman in the picture on the bottom left-hand corner is in a *cheongsam* made of Kelantan Silk.

that *batik cheongsam* became prevalent in the 1960s. While Mrs Lim had one made regularly every year, Mdm Lau had her only *batik cheongsam* tailored because she was given the fabric by a friend. The popularity of *batik* as a fabric for *cheongsam* could possibly be due to the mass production of *batik* from the 1950s onwards and the influence of popular films. *Batik* artist Mr Shahrul Said explained, "The period after the war can be seen as the industrial age of *batiks* when they were being mass-produced ... First there was the popular culture – the P. Ramlee shows ... Stamps were being invented and produced. After the war, with increased affluence, there was a demand for *batiks* and people were able to mass-produce ... So you have production and you have traders selling – the *batik* industry grew."[37] This phenomenon of consuming mass-produced *batik* in local fashion was similarly reflected in its use for other types of garments such as the Western dress and the tight-fitting modern *sarong kebaya* of the same period. Besides *batik*, other local fabrics that were used to make *cheongsam* included Kelantan Silk or Songket[38] and the printed georgette, American chiffon and nylex[39] favoured by Indian women for their *sari*. The use of fabrics that were distinctive to the Southeast Asian region in the Singapore *cheongsam* demonstrated that women had the ability to create a new set of aesthetics which distinguished them as trendy and modern in the society they lived in.

ABOVE: Details of *batik cheongsam*, 1960s.

OPPOSITE: *Cheongsam* made of mass-produced *batik* were quite common in Singapore by the 1960s. Sleeveless *cheongsam*, 1960s; *cheongsam* with capped sleeves and bolero jacket, late 1960s; *batik cheongsam* with capped sleeves, late 1960s; sleeveless *batik cheongsam* with matching long-sleeved jacket, 1960s.

A brown-and-white sleeveless jersey *cheongsam* with Optical Art motifs, 1960s.

This black ankle-length brocade *cheongsam* was the uniform of Chinese flight attendants of the Belgian airline SABENA, 1974.

Sleeveless *batik cheongsam*, 1960s.

Printed silk georgette *cheongsam* with silver sequins and beads embroidered on it. It was worn with an orange slip, 1970s.

幸福

東風

東風

THE HAPPINESS PICTORIAL   MARCH 1960 NO. 52

91
東風畫報

EAST
PRESENTS THE EAST TO THE WORLD

141
東畫風報

EAST
PRESENTS THE EAST TO THE WORLD

東風

東風

東風

28
東風畫報

EAST
PRESENTS THE EAST TO THE WORLD

136
東風畫報

EAST
PRESENTS THE EAST TO THE WORLD

134
東風畫報

EAST
PRESENTS THE EAST TO THE WORLD

東風

東風

幸福

14
東風畫報

EAST

88
EAST
PRESENTS THE EAST TO THE WORLD

THE HAPPINESS PICTORIAL   NO. 57

Conclusion

In 1971, *The Straits Times* carried an article which noted the decline in popularity of the *cheongsam* amongst the young.[45] The figure-hugging *cheongsam*, popular as a symbol of modernity, was now labelled as impractical and a hindrance to movement by younger women. It was also deemed old-fashioned as it was commonly seen on mothers and the older generation. With the onslaught of affordable ready-to-wear mass-produced Western garments at boutiques which had sprung up by the late 1960s, women's wardrobes were no longer limited by lack of choice. *Cheongsam* tailors faced stiff competition because firstly it had become more expensive to tailor the dress; and secondly, women were no longer willing to spend time at the tailor for fittings. Despite the gradual decline of the *cheongsam* in the early 1970s, one cannot deny that the garment had served the purposes of working women in Singapore well for the previous two decades. The dramatic change in identity experienced by women during the immediate post-war years, brought about by political and economic mobilisation, created an urgent need for them to find an appropriate garment that could best reflect their identities. A combination of factors, such as the assimilation of Western fashion, the introduction of new synthetic fabrics and the creativity and resourcefulness of women who established a set of new aesthetics as consumers and producers of fashion, helped to anchor the *cheongsam* as an everyday dress without being replaced by the Western garments of those times. Although it had reached a low point in its popularity by the 1970s, it would re-emerge in the 1990s in a different context and catering to a new set of customers.

[1]

[2]

The Cheongsam for All Occasions

The enduring nature of the *cheongsam* as an everyday dress in the modern woman's wardrobe could be further explained by its versatility as a dress for all occasions. Depending on the fabric and length, *cheongsam* could be worn to work, an afternoon tea party or a wedding dinner. For example, plain or printed cotton knee-length *cheongsam* were preferred as daywear while lace, silk, brocade, embellished or embroidered ankle-length *cheongsam* were reserved for formal events. Of these variations,

[4]

[3]

[5]

1. Ms Lim Kim Lian Veronica was featured in an advertisement wearing a tight-fitting *cheongsam*, late 1950s to early 1960s.

2. Miss Rotary 1952 dressed in a *cheongsam*. Besides Western gowns and the *sarong kebaya*, the other favourite dress worn by participants in beauty pageants was the *cheongsam*.

3. A group of female students graduating from the Sylvia Kho School, late 1950s. Mrs Sylvia Kho was one of Singapore's earliest wedding-dress designers in the 1950s. She not only ran her own bridal salon but also taught women dress-making skills.

6. Ladies waiting to be interviewed as receptionists and guides for the Singapore Constitution Exposition, 1959.

4. A bride wearing a gold brocade wedding *cheongsam* with her bridegroom, 1960s.

5. Miss Singapore pageant, 1962. The runner-up wore a high-slit ankle-length *cheongsam* which revealed her long legs.

7. The first accountants who graduated from Singapore Polytechnic included four men and one woman, 1961.

8. Receptionists selected for the Singapore Constitution Exposition at Kallang dressed in figure-hugging *cheongsam* trying on shoes given to them, 1959.

9. Mrs Nancy Lim in a cooking demonstration dressed in a tight-fitting *cheongsam*, 1965.

1. According to *The Straits Times*, the way to brighten up the black *cheongsam* during Chinese New Year is to wear it with a pair of matching red earrings, black gloves and shoes, 1960.

2. A model wears a black-and-white grosgrain *cheongsam* in a fashion show staged in Hong Kong, 1962.

the black *cheongsam* was probably the most enthralling and glamorous to the women of the 1950s and 1960s.

In Singapore, the wearing of black *cheongsam* by women as day and evening wear became more widespread in the 1950s because of modernisation and Westernisation. Black – previously considered inappropriate and taboo because of its symbolic associations with death, evil, tragedy and seduction[40] – became a staple in women's wardrobes. As women looked to fashion centres in Europe and Asia for inspiration, not only was black found in Western dresses but it was also incorporated into the *cheongsam*. It was widely reported in the papers and local fashion magazines that black was in vogue in fashion capitals such as Paris, Italy, New York and London. By the 1960s, a black *cheongsam* was believed to be the best investment a busy Singapore working woman could make. Extremely versatile and suitable for day or evening functions if matched with the right accessories, it became an attractive and affordable wardrobe option. Hence, the idea of the black *cheongsam* as a symbol of modernity gradually became entrenched in the increasingly cosmopolitan mindset of Singapore women.

3

3. Studio portrait of Mrs Nancy Lim in a black *cheongsam*, matching gloves and shoes, 1967.

4. Studio portrait of Mdm Wu Chuen Chuen in a sleeveless black *cheongsam* decorated with floral motifs, 1960s.

5. Mrs Nancy Lim dancing the cha-cha-cha in a black *cheongsam* embellished with the motifs of dragon and phoenix, 1958.

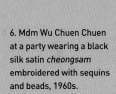

[5]

[4]

6. Mdm Wu Chuen Chuen at a party wearing a black silk satin *cheongsam* embroidered with sequins and beads, 1960s.

To overcome social conventions of dressing appropriately for formal functions, women managed to incorporate black creatively into their wardrobe for smart, elegant and formal wear. Black *cheongsam* were usually embellished with sequins or printed with floral and auspicious motifs such as the dragon and phoenix. It was also common to find black *cheongsam* with colourful embroidery or offset by bright colours such as gold to break its harsh look. Colourful accessories that dazzled, such as jewellery and clutch bags decorated with diamantes, also helped to liven up the black ensemble.[41]

[6]

Ankle-length gold
brocade bridal
cheongsam decorated
with large flower
buttons, 1960s.

Cheongsam with gold sequinned dragons were a popular evening outfit amongst Singapore women in the late 1950s and 1960s. The dragon signified strength, power and good luck in Chinese mythology. The tailor used black as a canvas to showcase his artwork of an entire dragon amongst clouds, using sequins and beads which he painstakingly embroidered by hand. This dress belongs to Mdm Wu Chuen Chuen.

TOP LEFT: A model at a fashion show at the St Andrew's Cathedral Memorial Hall, 1959.

TOP RIGHT: Mrs Nancy Lim was inspired by Chinese actress Chang Chung Wen (张仲文) and liked to style her hair to one side, 1966. Singapore women often got their fashion ideas from popular actresses on the silver screen.

FAR RIGHT: Studio portrait of Mrs Nancy Lim in a striped *cheongsam* which further elongated her body and created a pencil-slim look, 1964.

BOTTOM: Both Mdm Wu (left) and her friend are dressed in extremely figure-revealing mid-calf length cheongsam, late 1950s to early 1960s. The high-heeled shoes they are wearing help to accentuate their pencil-slim silhouettes.

THE CHEONGSAM AS A FORM OF CONTROL

Interestingly, some women considered the form-fitting *cheongsam* of the 1950s and 1960s to be an effective tool for controlling their bodies. Mrs Nancy Lim revealed how the *cheongsam* helped to discipline her body and kept her in shape:

> The *cheongsam* is like a corset and a weight-control garment because it is tight-fitting. Thus even after giving birth to three sons, I could still wear the *cheongsam*.[42]

Like Mrs Nancy Lim, Ms Mary Ann Chong also used the *cheongsam* as a means to keep her body trim and would go on a diet whenever she could not fit into one.[43] Perhaps it was the alluring notion of wanting to be feminine that made women wear the *cheongsam*. Master Lok Chye Kwai summarised this best: "The tight silhouette enhanced her femininity and gracefulness especially when the wearer moved",[44] which reinforced existing notions of the female body as feminine and how the body should behave. Ironically, it was the restrictions imposed by the tight-fitting *cheongsam* on the movement of the woman's body that made it lose its appeal by the beginning of the 1970s.

Singapore women after the war were beginning to place more emphasis on their appearance in conjunction with their changing roles in society. They would wear a corset or go on a diet in order to fit into a tight-fitting *cheongsam* like this one.

PROMINENT WOMEN

Prominent Women

espite having fallen out of favour by the 1970s, the *cheongsam* made a comeback in the 1990s. Singaporean sociologist Chua Beng Huat details its re-emergence to the fore in the following excerpt from his chapter titled "On the Power *Cheongsam* and Other Ethnic Clothes", which appeared in his book *Life is Not Complete Without Shopping: Consumption Culture in Singapore*, in 2003:

Opposite: Then Prime Minister Mr Lee Kuan Yew attending the National Day Reception hosted by then President Yusof Ishak at the Istana. He was accompanied by Mrs Lee who was dressed in a capped-sleeved printed *cheongsam* that reached down to her calves, 1960.

Page 76: Mrs Elizabeth Choy dressed in a silk damask *cheongsam* with flowers in her hair, 1955.

Page 77: Mrs Wee Kim Wee at then President Yusof Ishak's house, Sri Melati, Istana, 1968. Her blue lace *cheongsam* was accessorised with a brooch.

From the early 1990s, the *cheongsam* began to be a palpable presence on public formal occasions. It is true that for some Chinese women, for example Mrs Lee Kuan Yew and novelist Catherine Lim, the *cheongsam* is the exclusive dress for all formal occasions big or small, including business meetings. What is significant is that women educated in English, locally and abroad, had hitherto seldom, or never, been seen in a *cheongsam*, but now began to attend public, formal occasions adorned in this clearly Chinese identity marker. Among the most obvious were wives of politicians and other significant power players in and out of government, and women who were significant in their own right, such as directors or heads of government or non-government institutions, senior lawyers in private practice, entrepreneurs and senior academics. The *cheongsam* emerged, under the Asianisation process, as power clothing for women with power or in close association with power. Meanwhile, it remained absent from everyday life and celebratory occasions, such as wedding banquets, among middle- and working-class Chinese women.

In its original form as a formal garment of Manchurian women in the Ching Dynasty, the *cheongsam* was a straight-cut dress that reached the ankles, with a high collar, and sleeves cut wide just above the wrist but narrowed towards the shoulder.

A slit was cut on each side of the dress and undergarments were worn to avoid displaying the lower limbs. After the collapse of the dynasty, the garment was popularly adopted in different guises in China. Influenced by the 'modernity' of the republican era, the *cheongsam* was reshaped and mixed and matched with various garments. For example, a version that was shortened as a top and worn with a 'western' skirt became common as a school uniform in urban areas. By the 1930s, it had stabilised in its present stylised form. Today, the *cheongsam* is a single piece, tight-fitting sheath dress, of varying length, "with a high cylindrical collar, with an opening at the front, from the middle of the collar, following the upper contour of the right breast to the armpit and down the side" (Lam, 1991:4). The opening is fastened with either cloth buttons or press-studs. Sleeves are of varying length, or may be omitted altogether. The slit on either side of the dress remains. The length of the slits depends on the tightness of fit, "the tighter it is the higher the cut", to facilitate movement "as well as a decorative means of showing shapely legs" (Lam, 1991:4).

The semiotics of the *cheongsam* are complex. It is the garment of choice for self-marking as a Chinese; like "the kimono for Japan and the sari for India, the cheongsam has served to designate the Chinese women to the West" (Fairservis, 1971:118). Other modulations of self-representation are embedded in this generalised ethnic marker. Depending on the context in which it is donned, the degree of 'body consciousness' of the fit, the length or depth of the slits and the age, social class and status of the wearer, the meaning of the garment ranges from sleazy to elegant and respectable. At the sleazy extreme is that most Orientalist image of the Chinese prostitute, *a la* 'The World of Suzie Wong', or of a low-status Chinese restaurant waitress; such images continue to be used in Singapore in advertising posters for beer, brandy or stout found pasted in local coffee shops. At its most respectable it is associated with Chinese school teachers etched in every Singaporean's memories of student days. Thus, stylised representations of women in *cheongsam* are not entirely fictive.

The *cheongsam*'s presence had greatly diminished during the 1970s and 1980s, the period of rapid economic growth in Singapore. Labour force demand drew increasing

numbers of women into the job market, while the ideological dimensions of economic modernisation spilled into the cultural practices of the population. In such circumstances, the *cheongsam* all but disappeared from the everyday life of Chinese women, replaced by company uniforms or 'office' attire. The noticeable few exceptions stood out, precisely for their difference. Moreover, clothes were increasingly bought off-the-rack in the mushrooming shopping centres and department stores, replacing the earlier practice of home dress-making. By the mid-1980s, few young Chinese Singaporean women could imagine themselves in a *cheongsam* (Lam, 1991).

The visible re-emergence of the *cheongsam* as 'power clothing' for Chinese women is thus a 1990s phenomenon, coinciding with the impressive economic development of the past four decades that lifted Singapore from the despondency of underdevelopment to a per capita income higher than almost every nation in Europe. This rise of local affluence was jump-started by globalised capital in search of inexpensive production platforms, under what is now known as the new international division of labour. However, Singapore has since the 1980s moved beyond being a production site for low-end consumer commodities to become a capital-intensive centre for high technology industrialisation, with a greatly expanded financial and capital market.

Nevertheless, according to official discourse, this rise in affluence has been achieved by 'bootstrapping' the 'traditional' values of the people. For the Chinese, this meant a Confucian emphasis on hard work, education, pragmatism and family cohesion, values that have been ideologically distilled into a set of 'Asian values'. (This is, of course, a very narrow reading of the cultural underpinning of capitalism for it has screened out the routinised cultural demands and practices of a proletarianised population reduced to the status of wage labour, albeit on different scales and incomes.[1]) The *cheongsam* for Chinese women of power in Singapore in the 1990s became a symbolic expression of Chinese-ness, of Chinese values as constitutive parts of 'Asian values'. On occasions graced or tinted with cabinet ministerial presence, hence the presence of power and official ideology, it represents acquiescence to, if not affirmation of, the national ideology.

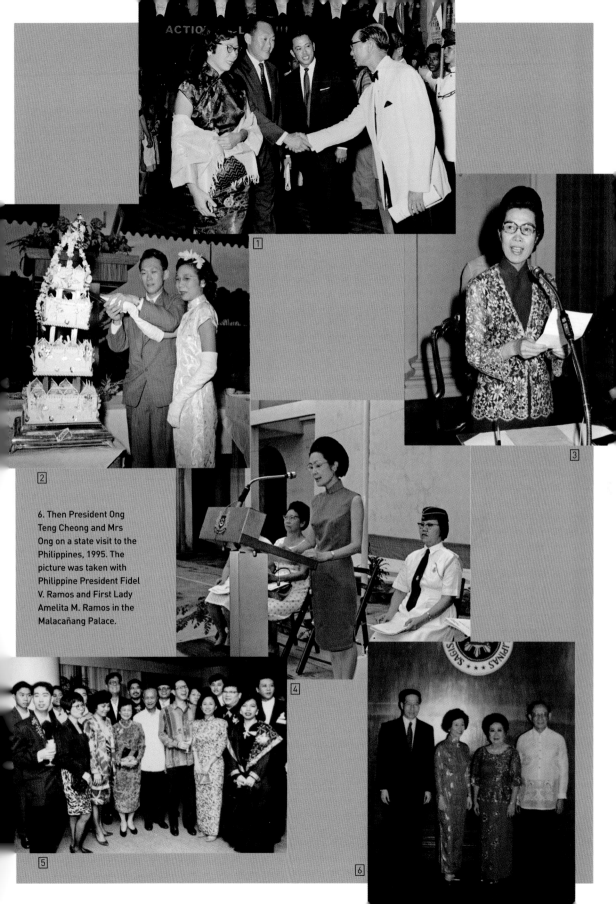

[1]

[2]

[3]

6. Then President Ong
Teng Cheong and Mrs
Ong on a state visit to the
Philippines, 1995. The
picture was taken with
Philippine President Fidel
V. Ramos and First Lady
Amelita M. Ramos in the
Malacañang Palace.

[4]

[5]

[6]

LEFT: Sleeveless silk *cheongsam* with *batik* motifs and black piping, 1990s. This *cheongsam*, belonging to Mrs Lee Kuan Yew, came with a matching shawl.

OPPOSITE: Sleeveless brocade ankle-length *cheongsam* in gold. Mrs Lee Kuan Yew wore this *cheongsam* on several occasions, such as the 80th birthday of Mr Lee Kuan Yew in 2003.

Mrs Elizabeth Choy/Yong Ju-Moi (1910–2006)

Mrs Elizabeth Choy was born Yong Su-Moi in Kudat, North Borneo, to a Hakka Chinese family. She received an English education at the Convent of the Holy Infant Jesus in Singapore in 1929 and married Choy Khun Heng in 1941.[2]

During the Japanese Occupation, Mr and Mrs Choy ran a canteen at the predecessor to the Woodbridge Hospital and secretly passed on food, medicine, money and messages for European civilians and prisoners-of-war (POWs) interned at Changi. They even smuggled in radio parts so the internees could build a secret radio set. Eventually the Japanese suspected them of being involved in the raid on Singapore Harbour in September 1943 and both Mr and Mrs Choy were arrested and tortured by the *Kempetai* (the Japanese military police). After 193 days of imprisonment, she was finally released. After the war, she was honoured as a war heroine and was awarded with the Order of the British Empire (OBE) with her husband by King George VI (r. 1936–1952). She participated in Singapore's politics from 1950 to 1955.[3] Mrs Choy represented a small but growing number of Singapore women who were no longer shy about getting their voices heard in matters related to nation-building.

Mrs Choy often represented Singapore at overseas events. For example, in 1953, she attended the coronation of Queen Elizabeth II and was invited to speak about Singapore and Malaysia in North America.[4] During these occasions, she left a deep impression on her foreign hosts as the Oriental woman clad in form-fitting *cheongsam*. Mrs Choy liked to inject her own style when dressing up, such as adorning her hair with ornaments made with flowers and wearing fine braided bracelets.[5] For the Queen's coronation, she even had an ivory silk satin *cheongsam* specially made that was decorated with a dragon motif and the Chinese characters for "Long Live the Queen; may there be universal peace" embroidered on it.[6] At home, she was also popularly known as the "the Dayak Woman of Singapore"[7] as a reference to her short fringe, dark complexion, athletic frame and her preference for *batik cheongsam*.

LEFT: Singapore Legislative Councillor Mrs Elizabeth Choy presenting certificates of competency to nurses and hospital assistants at the Singapore General Hospital, 1954.

OPPOSITE:
1. Mrs Elizabeth Choy teaching at St Andrew's School, 1953.

2. Mrs Elizabeth Choy presenting a nursing certificate to a male nurse, 1954.

3. Mrs Elizabeth Choy and her children at home, 1953.

4. Mrs Elizabeth Choy opening the new school building of the Convent of the Holy Infant Jesus (CHIJ), 1952.

5. Mrs Elizabeth Choy and Minister for Culture S. Rajaratnam watching a performance by blind children during a Christmas party at Radio Singapore, 1959. Mrs Choy was in a *batik cheongsam*.

1

2

3

4

5

LEFT: Silk satin *cheongsam* with a dragon embroidered with gold, silver and red thread. This *cheongsam* belonged to Mrs Elizabeth Choy.

OPPOSITE: Silk satin *cheongsam* with capped sleeves and motifs of floral bouquets painted on it. This was one of the *cheongsam* worn by Mrs Elizabeth Choy when she was in London for the coronation of Queen Elizabeth II, 1953.

Datin Aw Cheng Hu (1914–2010)

Datin Aw Cheng Hu was born in Rangoon, Burma (now Myanmar). She came to Singapore at the age of 13 when her father, Mr Aw Boon Par, decided to re-locate his business, Eng Aun Tong, from Burma to Singapore.[8] In 1931, Mdm Aw married Dato Lee Chee San who was subsequently appointed the Managing Director of the family bank, Chung Khiaw Bank, in 1950.

Datin Aw led an extremely busy life filled with openings, luncheons and dinners related to her husband's business.[9] She not only accompanied Dato Lee overseas to scout for new premises for their banks but also travelled extensively for leisure.

Dato Lee was raised in a traditional Chinese family and was extremely particular about the appearance of his staff and what they wore to work. His staff needed to be neat rather than trendy,[10] and he felt that the *cheongsam* epitomised this quality best. He banned his female staff at Chung Khiaw from wearing Western dresses to work. Instead they had to wear the traditional one-piece dress and this was also extended to his family including his wife. According to May Chu, their granddaughter, "Mamak [Datin Aw] always dressed as he [Dato Lee] wished – colourfully, in traditional Chinese *cheongsam*, always with matching red lipstick and nail polish. Each *cheongsam* had its own matching set of jewellery – nothing subdued ever, not even during the day."[11]

Datin Aw was fond of colourful lace *cheongsam* matched with short cropped jackets. She also preferred fabrics with psychedelic prints which were popular in the late 1960s and 1970s. She shopped at Modern Silk Store, Metro, Majeed or Chotirmall at High Street and tailored her *cheongsam* at the high-end Eastern Paris Gown Shop at St Gregory's Place in Singapore.[12]

TOP LEFT: Datin Aw Cheng Hu attending a cocktail party at Victoria Memorial Hall, 1960. A brooch on the collar helped her *cheongsam* look more glamorous.

MIDDLE: Datin Aw Cheng Hu receiving a bouquet at the opening of the "Disneyland" attraction at Kallang Park, 1969.

TOP RIGHT: Datin Aw Cheng Hu at the opening of the Hyatt Hotel, 1971.

RIGHT: Orange-and-gold floral *cheongsam* in French lace and a matching jacket. The scalloped hemming found on the collar, cuff of the sleeves and hem of the jacket was extremely popular in the late 1960s.

FOLLOWING PAGES: Datin Aw Cheng Hu preferred *cheongsam* with sleeves and a matching jacket. They were usually made of French lace or jersey in various printed designs popular in the late 1960s and early 1970s.

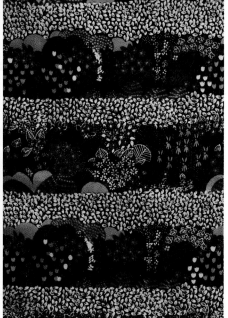

LEFT: Details of floral *cheongsam*, late 1960s.

OPPOSITE LEFT: Ankle-length sleeveless blue *cheongsam* with water-coloured floral motifs in silk georgette, late 1960s to early 1970s.

OPPOSITE RIGHT: Mrs Irene Lim had a preference for fabrics with horizontal panels because it helped her look less skinny. Sleeveless *cheongsam* with various horizontal motifs, 1970s.

Mrs Irene Lim (b. 1927–)

Mrs Irene Lim was born in Kuala Lumpur, Malaysia, to a Peranakan family and they settled down in Singapore in 1928. She received an English education at Raffles Girls' School from 1934 to 1941 – a result of her father's wish for her to speak proper English.[13] Mrs Lim was exposed to the *cheongsam* from a very young age by her mother Ms Edna Kung, who was often dressed in a chic *cheongsam*. Her mother also contributed regularly to a fashion column in *The Straits Times*.[14] Initially, Mrs Lim wore the *cheongsam* to assert her identity as a Chinese. She explained, "I was dark-skinned and had frizzy hair. Everyone calls me an Eurasian. I wanted to be Chinese and so I wore the *cheongsam*."[15] Later she found the one-piece dress extremely convenient to wear because "it never goes out of fashion" and did not require her to mix and match, unlike other outfits. Besides, she discovered that the form-fitting *cheongsam* kept her slim all these years.[16]

Mrs Lim considered the collar the most beautiful part of the *cheongsam*. She liked it high because it accentuated her slender neck. According to her, a good tailor should be able to cut the collar so that it does not hinder the movement of the wearer. Most of her *cheongsam* were made of silk or Swiss cotton because she was allergic to certain fabrics such as synthetics. Hence, she would often rub the fabric against her skin to test for irritation before purchasing it. She found fabrics that were printed with horizontal motifs more flattering to wear because of her small frame and thus they featured prominently in her wardrobe.

LEFT: Mdm Zhuo Yu Chun in a short-sleeved *cheongsam* printed with swirls and fan-like motifs, 1952.

OPPOSITE:

1. Mdm Zhuo and her husband at a party, 1952. Mdm Zhuo loved to decorate her *cheongsam* with a prominent flower.

2. Mdm Zhuo (right) and a friend on a cruise ship, early 1950s.

3. Mdm Zhuo (second from right) in Penang, 1951.

4. Mdm Zhuo (right) in Hong Kong, 1956.

5. Mdm Zhuo dressed in a short-sleeved loose-fitting *cheongsam*, late 1940s.

6. Mdm Zhuo in Bali, 1952.

MDM ZHUO YU CHUN (B. 1920–)

Mdm Zhuo Yu Chun was born in Bagan Siapiapi[17] on the northern coast of Sumatra. Her father was a Chinese immigrant who married a local. Being Indonesian Chinese, Mdm Zhuo was proud of her Chinese heritage and felt that the *cheongsam* represented her Chinese identity.[18] She described it as "a demure and dignified garment"[19] and wore her first *cheongsam* at 17 when she became a schoolteacher in Bagan.

Shortly after the Second World War, she settled down in Singapore with her husband Mr Koh Tin Kok. In 1956, they established Kim Way Local Products Company, which distributed frozen food imported from China to Singapore, and San Yi Film, which re-distributed films from China and Hong Kong. As a result, Mdm Zhuo often had to play host to guests from the food business and the film industry and soon her wardrobe of *cheongsam* expanded rapidly to suit her changing lifestyle.

Mdm Zhuo's wardrobe consisted mainly of ankle-length silk damask *cheongsam* in various colours. They were often decorated with elaborate flower buttons or brocade panels sewn separately onto the dress. For business meetings, she preferred the *cheongsam* with a Western-style jacket. She had hers made only in Hong Kong as she believed that the tailors there were more skilled than those in Singapore and they were often ahead of fashion trends. Most of the fabrics were purchased abroad, especially in Hong Kong, although some were from High Street in Singapore. A few of Mdm Zhuo's *cheongsam* have matching shawls which reminded her of her grandmother's *selandang* (shoulder cloth).

Floral *cheongsam* with matching jackets in silk, 1960s. Mdm Zhuo's *cheongsam* and jackets were often characterised by intricate floral buttons handmade by Shanghainese tailors in Hong Kong.

OPPOSITE FROM LEFT TO RIGHT: Silk damask ankle-length *cheongsam* with long sleeves, late 1960s; silk floral *cheongsam* with matching shawl, late 1960s; silk damask *cheongsam* with red and gold piping, late 1960s; black silk damask *cheongsam* with brocade panel, late 1960s.

Mrs Christina Loke/Christina Lee Hui Wong (1923–2009)

Christina Lee was born in Singapore to a well-to-do family.[20] She received her education in Australia and America[21] before she married Cathay cinema tycoon Dato Loke Wan Tho in 1950.

Lee had always led an active social life. Even before her marriage, she was often spotted at public events. She also loved sports and was an avid golfer.[22] In the 1950s, as Dato Loke expanded his business into restaurants and hotels, Lee was increasingly seen at charity events, company luncheons, dinners and film festivals. She also accompanied her husband on his business trips overseas.

Lee was known for her beauty and poise and was frequently photographed by the media in her *cheongsam*. For evening functions, she preferred silk, brocade, velvet or embroidered sleeveless *cheongsam*. Sometimes, she wore them with a silk stole. When she travelled, she would complement her *cheongsam* with a Western-style overcoat. Renowned Singapore artist Cheong Soo Pieng and Indonesian painter Basoeki Abdullah had painted portraits of the elegant Lee dressed in her stylish *cheongsam* in the late 1940s and 1950s. In 1965, American fashion magazine *Vogue* even listed her as one of the 10 most beautiful women in the world. Lee and Dato Loke divorced in 1962.

Lee was also an accomplished photographer and entrepreneur. She was recognised for her photography of birds[23] and published three books on the subject.[24] A keen art collector herself, Lee tried to revive Borneo pottery in the mid-1960s and sold pieces in a shop at the Shangri-La Hotel. In 1973, she founded the Perfumes of Singapore business with her then husband, Dr Dadi Balsara, and created home-grown scents such as "The Singapore Girl" and "Christina". Lee passed away in 2009 and a year later, a chest full of jackets and *cheongsam* in wool and velvet, most probably worn during her overseas trips, was discovered and donated to the National Museum of Singapore.

Sleeveless grey *cheongsam* with vertical embroidered floral panel in red.

Sleeveless grey *cheongsam* with lozenge prints.

Sleeveless black *cheongsam* in velvet with red roses.

Mrs Wee Kim Wee/Mdm Koh Sok Hiong (1916–)

Mrs Wee Kim Wee was born Koh Sok Hiong to a Peranakan family in Singapore.[25] She was Chinese-educated and studied at Hwa Chiau Chinese and English School in Pasir Panjang (1924–1932), then at Nanyang Girls' High School before she married Mr Wee Kim Wee in 1934 and became a full-time housewife. Mr Wee later became the President of Singapore from 1985 to 1993.[26]

Mrs Wee was well-known for her culinary skills which she picked up from her grandmother from the age of 10. In 1965, she contributed a series of *nonya* recipes for the column "Malaysian Kitchen" in *Her World*, a leading local English-language fashion magazine established in 1960. With these skills and a warm personality, she was always a confident and hospitable host. During Mr Wee's appointment as High Commissioner to Malaysia (1973–1980) and subsequently as Ambassador to Japan and the Republic of Korea (1980–1984), guests enjoyed dinner parties and receptions that featured Mrs Wee's delicious *nonya* dishes. Sylvia Toh, who was Mr Wee's personal assistant from 1980 to 1983, noted that for Mrs Wee, "cooking and managing a formal sit-down official dinner for 20 guests was just as easy as preparing for a one-to-one lunch ... she could even cook for Singapore's National Day reception for 500 to 600 guests and the reception for about 200 Singapore students the following day."[27]

When Mr Wee became President, Mrs Wee's role took on an additional dimension. She regularly accompanied the President on overseas state visits. She also had to play hostess to foreign heads of state and their spouses on their visits to Singapore. At home, she had to attend numerous public engagements where she was either the guest of honour or patron.

Mrs Wee was always elegantly dressed in a *cheongsam* at public events. It was first observed that she began to wear the *cheongsam* more than the *sarong kebaya* when she and Mr Wee took up ballroom dancing in the early 1950s. The *cheongsam*, with slits at the sides, was more convenient for moving on the dance floor.[28] By the time Mr Wee was appointed ambassador, Mrs Wee had a wardrobe full of *cheongsam* in different fabrics and styles for various occasions. During the day, she would put on a *cheongsam* that ended slightly below the knee, matched with a jacket, while lace or silk chiffon ankle-length *cheongsam* were preferred for evening functions. Many of her *cheongsam* were in red, her favourite colour.

ABOVE LEFT: Mrs Wee Kim Wee making the final preparations for a reception at the Singapore embassy in Tokyo, early 1980s.

ABOVE RIGHT: Mr and Mrs Wee Kim Wee dancing during their diamond (60th) wedding anniversary dinner, 1996. Mrs Wee was dressed in her favourite red *cheongsam*.

LEFT: Ankle-length apricot *cheongsam* in lace, late 1980s. Mrs Wee wore this *cheongsam* when Queen Elizabeth II visited Singapore in 1989.

PAGE 108: Ankle-length red *cheongsam* in silk chiffon with vertical silver thread. Mrs Wee Kim Wee wore this for the President's birthday celebration in 1992.

PAGE 109: Sleeveless yellow *cheongsam* in lace with matching V-neck long-sleeved jacket with scalloped hem. Yellow was one of Mrs Benjamin Sheares' favourite colours.

THE PRODUCERS OF CHEONGSAM

The Producers of *Cheongsam*

Traditionally, the *cheongsam* as a fitted garment made it necessary to be custom-made. This chapter examines the background of the *cheongsam* tailors and their contributions to the development of the garment in Singapore. The fate of these tailors, many of them from Shanghai, was intertwined with the evolving meaning of the *cheongsam* and the changing lifestyles of the women who wore it. The business of these tailors peaked during the post-war period but had declined by the 1970s as a result of competition from department stores and mass-produced Western garments. By the 1980s, many of them had retired and there was little interest among the younger generation to learn and continue their craft. In recent years, however, another group of *cheongsam* producers has emerged, comprising both young and established fashion designers and cultural entrepreneurs. As a result of their attempts to give a modern interpretation to the traditional *cheongsam*, they have helped to rejuvenate it and extend its relevance and longevity as a choice of dress in the wardrobe of the modern Singapore woman.

OPPOSITE: A lace *cheongsam* designed by Priscilla Shunmugam, 2011. The dress is embellished with vintage buttons sourced by the designer to give it a more unusual look and it is worn with a pair of red high-heeled shoes.

PAGE 110: Mrs Nancy Lim in a sleeveless lace *cheongsam* with a pair of fashionable wedge sandals, 1955.

PAGE 111: A modern interpretation of the *batik cheongsam* by cultural entrepreneur Tan Sheau Yun. The *cheongsam* ends above the knee and the fabric is printed with bold fish motifs with a netted background.

Shanghai as the Fashion Capital

The most skilled *cheongsam* tailors were associated with Shanghai.[1] It became a treaty port in 1842, and by the early 20th century, Shanghai had developed so rapidly that it overtook Guangzhou as China's most popular commercial centre for European traders.[2] As a result of its development, foreign companies mushroomed in Shanghai and soon the cosmopolitan city became the meeting place between Eastern and Western cultures, ideas and fashion. At the same time, a

group of resourceful and skilful Ningbo tailors called the *Feng Bang Cai Feng* (奉帮裁缝), from the northeast of Zhejiang Province, migrated to Shanghai in the late 19th century. These tailors saw the potential for custom-made Western garments with the influx of foreign staff working in Shanghai and the pursuit of Western fashion by wealthy locals. Soon, they incorporated Western techniques into their practice, including the *cheongsam*, and they became sought after by foreigners and locals who preferred Western garb. As a result, the Ningbo tailors became known as the *Hong Bang Cai Feng* (红帮裁缝).[3]

The term "Shanghainese tailor" referred to those who learnt their craft in Shanghai. According to Master Lok Chye Kwai, Shanghainese tailors could be from Yangzhou, Guangzhou, Suzhou or Fuzhou.[4] Master Hou Sing elaborated this further, "There is a man called Liu Bao Jin and he teaches people how to tailor clothes … He is from Fuzhou but he learnt how to tailor in a Shanghainese school. A lot of people say he is Shanghainese but he can barely speak the dialect."[5] In short, one did not have to be Shanghainese to qualify as a Shanghainese tailor.

The Apprentice

In China, teenagers who were not academically inclined were sent to learn a skill by their families. Many apprentices started at the age of 12 and the length of training varied from three to five years. *Ben Bang* (本帮) tailors took three years and specialised only in making traditional Chinese clothing which included making the *cheongsam*, piping and flower buttons. *Hong Bang* (红帮) tailors, mentioned above, required five years of apprenticeship because they were taught to make Chinese, Western and winter garments. Master Lok, who was trained as a *Hong Bang* tailor, claimed that although the training was longer, "you would be able to make all the clothes in the world if you mastered the skills."[6] Hence, *Hong Bang* tailors seemed to have an edge over *Ben Bang* tailors.

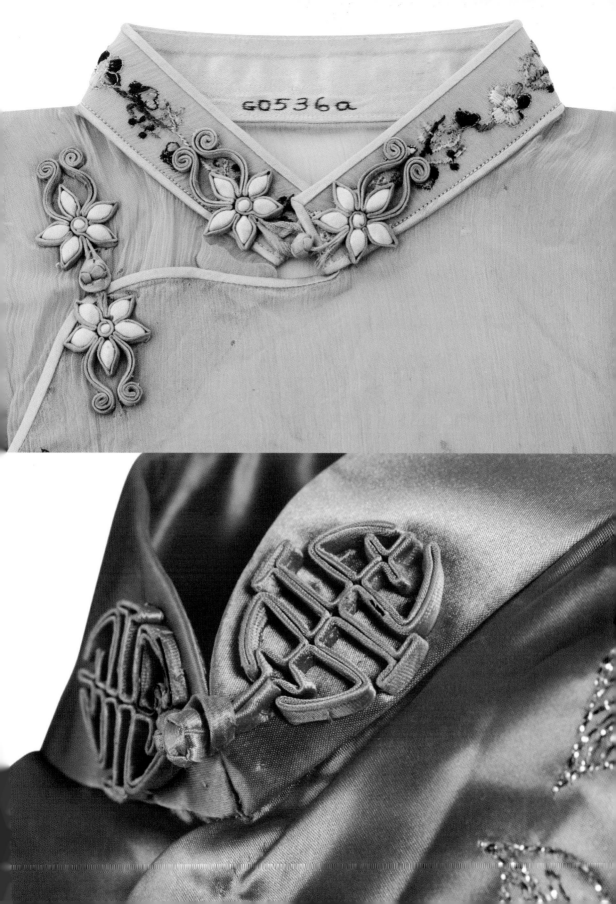

An apprentice was accepted only by recommendation. Upon confirmation, an agreement was signed between the trainee and the Master Tailor. It stated that if the former did not complete his training, his family had to compensate the latter for all of the apprentice's expenses, such as food and lodging. Sometimes, a guarantor was required. Women were not accepted as apprentices although they were involved in embroidery work and simple tasks.

Life as an apprentice was tough. The day started at 6.00am and ended at 11.30pm. Besides learning the basic skills of sewing, he was also expected to cook breakfast, wash the dishes and run errands for the Master.[7] At night, he slept on a mat on the floor or the worktable in the shop and received only 20 cents per month (in China's currency then) for a hair cut. There was no day off and the situation would only improve when a new apprentice was recruited two to three years later. Hence, it was not unusual that there were apprentices who ran away from their Master before completing their training. However, Master Lok noted that being an apprentice in Singapore was better, for example, he was allowed to rest on Sunday evenings.

In order for an apprentice to succeed, he must be able to endure hardship and be patient and hardworking. Besides performing menial tasks, a trainee had to learn how to sew things by hand, which included buttons, hooks and lining. It could take up to three months before he could attain a steady hand in order to hold the needle.[8] The apprentice was normally taught by the junior tailor and not the Master Tailor. Master Hou explained, "The master would never teach us … because it would waste his time and he would want to earn money."[9] In order to improve one's skills, the apprentice had to observe the Master Tailor closely and take the initiative to ask questions. At the end of the fifth year, a hardworking apprentice would most likely be able to make an outfit even if he had not mastered all the skills. He could then choose either to continue working for his Master Tailor or work in another tailor's shop.

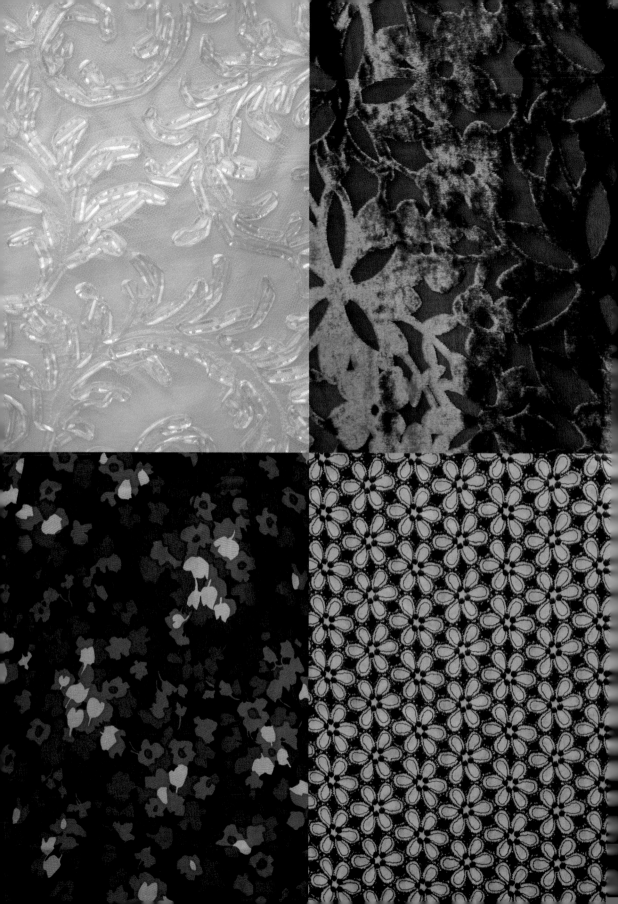

Shanghainese Tailors in Singapore

The first group of Shanghainese tailors probably arrived in Singapore in the 1920s; one of them was Master Xu Jin Sheng who subsequently introduced other tailors to Singapore.[10] By the time Master Ching arrived in Singapore in 1936, there were already 10 tailor shops along Orchard Road owned by Shanghainese. Other areas dominated by tailors from Shanghai included the Indian shops on High Street and foreign-owned shops at Bukit Timah. However, the number of Shanghainese tailors in Singapore in the 1930s was still considered insignificant compared to the huge shops in Shanghai. The second wave of Shanghainese tailors arrived in Singapore in the late 1930s and 1940s with the outbreak of the Second Sino-Japanese War (1937–1945) and the Chinese Civil War (1946–1949). Many of them came by boat and would have stopped at Hong Kong for a few days before arriving in Singapore.

Most tailors came to Singapore in search of a better life. Master Lok explained, "I wanted to come to Nanyang [Singapore] because it was a place of the British. I was very young then and did not understand the concept of a colony. There were many foreigners in Shanghai and many of them owned cars and houses."[11] Hence at the age of 12, Master Lok came to Singapore with his Master Tailor. There were other factors. The intense competition amongst tailors in Shanghai and the lack of tailors in Singapore during the 1920s and 1930s led them to believe that they could do better here. Others like Master Hou wanted to see and explore the world when he was young.[12] However, most of them were disappointed when they arrived in Singapore. Master Ng realised, "Singapore was less developed than Shanghai as it had nothing."[13]

From the 1920s to the 1940s, the majority of the tailors in Singapore specialised in making Western garments for Europeans and Americans and not

星洲華人洋服工會敬贈

人洋服工會

勳章聯歡會一九五一年七月廿九日攝影留念

星洲華

慶祝名譽會長伍桑才先生榮膺帝國英皇

孫崇瑜先生惠存

Right: Mrs Nancy Lim
at a shop selling *batik*
fabrics, 1970.

Opposite: Details of a
variety of patterns found
on natural and synthetic
fabrics from the 1950s
to 1960s.

the *cheongsam*. Master Ng recounted, "Before the [Second World] war, no one made *qipao*. If they wanted to make *qipao*, they would go to Hong Kong ... Most of the *qipao* were personally brought over from China or Hong Kong if these women wanted to wear them in Singapore. There were no dedicated *qipao*-making tailors in Singapore. It was later when there was a demand for them that one or two of these tailors came over to Singapore."[14] In fact, Master Hou observed that most Chinese women wore the *samfoo*.[15] Those who wore the *cheongsam* were largely Chinese teachers who came from China, wealthy Chinese women including *nonyas* and girls from well-to-do families. Ms Tan Sock Kern recalled that her first two *cheongsam* were given to her as presents by her brothers who were studying in Hong Kong.[16] Tailors who specialised in making *cheongsam* did not own any shops as the demand was too small to sustain the business. Thus, Singapore women who wanted to have *cheongsam* made would visit more established Chinese-owned tailor shops, or were referred to a *cheongsam* tailor by the big tailor shops along High Street.[17]

Things only began to change after the Second World War when there was a surge in women who not only preferred to wear Western dresses but also traditional garments with a tighter fit. Master Lok attributed this phenomenon to the Westernisation and modernisation of Singapore women during the post-war period.[18] The changing silhouette of *cheongsam* from loose to tight not only signified a shift in women's role from traditional homemakers to working

LEFT: Detail of flower buttons on a lace *cheongsam*.

women but also marked a major turning point for the making of *cheongsam* and the development of *cheongsam* tailors in Singapore. Previously, the one-piece loose-cut *cheongsam* was done best by *Ben Bang* tailors. Now, *Hong Bang* tailors who were adept at making form-fitting Western evening gowns were in demand for their ability to transform the loose-cut *cheongsam* into a modern, fitted dress which accentuated the wearer's figure and femininity. As a result of an increase in women wearing *cheongsam*, many Shanghainese tailors trained in making Western garments, like Master Lok, began to specialise in making *cheongsam* in the 1950s.

Hong Kong and Singapore Tailors

It was often argued that Shanghainese tailors in Hong Kong were better at making *cheongsam* than those in Singapore. Several reasons were given for this. Firstly, shops in Hong Kong preferred to hire older tailors rather than younger ones, who had less experience. Master Hou observed, "The workmanship of Hong Kong tailors was better compared to those in Singapore and Europe. Usually the older tailors would be the ones giving instructions."[19] There were also more Shanghainese tailors in Hong Kong and the intense competition ensured that the *cheongsam* made were of better quality. During the 1940s, there was a mass exodus of Shanghainese tailors who left China for Hong Kong and beyond as a result of the Civil War at home. About 80 per cent of them remained in Hong Kong and they brought along their skills and the latest fashion trends. By the early 1950s, there were more than 600 Shanghainese tailors in Hong Kong.[20] Master Ching pointed out that the difference in weather between the two territories also had an impact on the skills of these tailors. "It is because of the warm weather. Hence they [the Singapore tailors] are not trained in producing fur or woollen coats. This makes for a huge difference in skill."[21]

Overall, the skills of Shanghainese tailors were considered the best amongst other Chinese tailors such as the Cantonese and the Hakkas. Master

RIGHT: Detail of the
stand-up collar of a
cheongsam in velvet with
burn-out pattern.

Hou explained, "For one thing, the training for Shanghainese tailors is harsher and they would need to devote more time into it. I feel that the workmanship of the Shanghainese tailors is better on the whole. Most of the time, the Cantonese, Hokkiens and Teochews would come to us to learn how to tailor."[22] Shanghainese tailors were not only taught how to sew everything by hand, they were also known for their ability to tailor the most fitted *cheongsam*. This was achieved by ironing and "pulling" the fabric repeatedly during the dress-making process. Master Ng clarified, "You had to iron the cloth after sewing, as it was not done so by the sewing machine ... You had to straighten the cloth out in order to maintain the fit of the garment."[23] Ironing was used to stretch and mould the silk around the bodice and hips to create three-dimensional effects.[24] Master Ng further elaborated on the advantage of sewing the dress by hand, "Even after washing the garment many times, the quality of the garment would not be compromised for at least three to five years."[25] Therefore, women preferred to have their *cheongsam* made by Shanghainese tailors because the dresses they made were of better quality and more durable.

Cheongsam Tailoring: An Art or a Science?

According to Master Lok, a good *cheongsam* tailor must be equipped with good taste and an eye for detail. Very often, the fabric of the *cheongsam* would feature embroidery or motifs. The tailor must be able to sew the different sections of a *cheongsam* together so as to create a symmetrical and aesthetically pleasing dress. For example, the motif, embroidery and colour on both sides of the collar should match seamlessly. In addition, while the front of the *cheongsam* should always look the best, an experienced tailor would make sure that the fabric motif or embroidery was coordinated on the front and back. To complete the *cheongsam*, the tailor also had to match the colours and design of the piping and flower buttons to the dress. In short, Master Lok described himself as an artist whose canvas was the *cheongsam*.[26]

LEFT: Studio photographs of two women in *cheongsam* embellished with embroidery.

OPPOSITE: Dato Loke Wan Tho and his wife, Christina Lee, arriving for the opening of New Hollywood Theatre, 1958. She is wearing a sleeveless mid-calf length *cheongsam* in silk and is carrying a clutch bag in her hands.

Another important aspect of *cheongsam*-making was the ability to take accurate measurements of the wearer. Every woman's figure is different and the tailor must know how to calculate the amount of excess fabric that had to be taken in at the bust, hips, waist and shoulders so that the *cheongsam* would fit her perfectly. Master Lok noted "Fittings are not necessary if you know how to take proper measurements ... To be accurate and fast, your mathematics must be good."[27] Thus, making a *cheongsam* is both an art and a science.

Significance of the *Cheongsam* to a Tailor

The tailors considered the traditional *cheongsam* as an ethnic marker of the Chinese woman that distinguished her from other Asian women. Master Hou explained, "Usually the wealthy would tailor it [the *cheongsam*] if they were going to Europe on business or if their husbands had some things to attend to there. The *qipao* is representative of Asian culture."[28] Master Lok pointed out further that a custom-made *cheongsam* was more suited for the petite Chinese woman compared to a Western dress.[29] Every woman could make a *cheongsam* that suited her needs and economic means. For example, working women could choose *cheongsam* made in affordable Chinese silk while society ladies would prefer more expensive European silk. As each *cheongsam* was tailor-made, there was also an exclusive quality which women, as consumers, appreciated. Thus, during the 1960s and 1970s, *cheongsam* was the preferred wear for society ladies at formal events.

成教局第三届高级缝剪班学員暨·周玲芳講師合影
1965 年 6月 7日摄

Women as Producers of Cheongsam

Traditionally, only men were accepted as apprentices by Shanghainese tailors. However, there were some women who were undeterred by this lack of formal training and made their own *cheongsam* so as to distinguish themselves from other women. Ms Tan Sock Kern learnt how to make a *cheongsam* from her mother and wore it to school while her friends wore Western frocks in the late 1930s.[35] After the Second World War, tailoring schools emerged, which taught women how to sew and make clothes. One such school was the Shanghai Nü Fu Xue Xi Suo (上海女服学习所).[36] In these classes, students were taught every month how to take measurements and sew different types of clothes including *cheongsam*. Mdm Chen Hui Ying, a former teacher, used to make her own *cheongsam* by following the basic pattern of the *sam*, the traditional blouse which looked like the *cheongsam* except that it ended at the waist or hips.[37] Later on, her relative who learnt tailoring from a Shanghainese tailor helped her to create a *cheongsam* paper pattern which she then used to make her *cheongsam*.

Top: The third batch of female graduates from Cheng Jiao Ju's Intermediate Tailoring and Sewing Class (成教局第三届高级缝剪班) and their guest lecturer Ms Zhou Ling Fang (centre), 7 June 1965.

Centre: Mrs Nancy Lim using a sewing machine, 1959. She is dressed in a tight-fitting *cheongsam*.

Below: Female students at the first anniversary of Ling Fang Intermediate Tailoring and Sewing School (玲芳高级剪裁学院周年庆典), 12 April 1965. Specialised schools to help women acquire tailoring and sewing skills began to emerge in the 1950s and 1960s. While these skills allowed some women to work from home and earn an income, for others, they allowed them to make their own clothes in the style that they liked.

A model walks the runway at the Vivienne Tam Fall 2007 fashion show. The modified *cheongsam* features prints inspired by esoteric Buddhism.

Decline of *Cheongsam* Tailors

By the 1970s, the business of *cheongsam* tailoring was beginning to decline. The *cheongsam* was losing its appeal amongst the younger generation as a form of daily wear and was replaced by ready-to-wear Western garments. There were also fewer and fewer Shanghainese tailors who made *cheongsam* in Singapore. Master Ng recounted, "The tailoring business is declining and we are getting older and are unable to remain competitive in the industry. People have education now and even if they were interested in the industry, they would pursue it abroad."[30] After the Second World War, there were hardly any apprentices who joined the trade because it was considered too tough and time-consuming. Master Ng reflected, "The younger generations are more interested in skills involving the use of machines, and they use models for designing. They would not learn the same way as we did in the past, where we had to learn everything from scratch. We relied on the experiences and skills of our masters as our learning method. Now, tailoring involves the specialisation of labour where people have different tasks in the process."[31]

The irregular and long working hours of a *cheongsam* tailor also discouraged people from learning the craft, especially the children of these tailors. Master Hou explained, "We have our busy periods and our lull periods. Sometimes we have customers bringing in five to six outfits that they wish to tailor within the next two days and so we will be busy."[32]

Master Ching also observed that the emphasis on education by the government after the war had an impact on the number of tailors in Singapore. In the early 20th century, most people were unable to afford an education in Shanghai and thus became apprentices to learn a trade. By the 1950s and 1960s, Singapore's quest for development and modernisation meant that education for children was encouraged. Thus, fewer and fewer people were interested in tailoring.

The high cost of starting a business was another daunting factor. Master Ching lamented, "I am old now, and my children have all graduated. I have no one to take over the business from me. It is the same situation for my friends and their

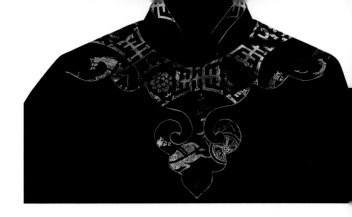

RIGHT: Detail of a brocade panel on a silk damask *cheongsam*, 1960s. The panel is decorated with auspicious motifs such as flowers, bats and the Chinese character for longevity (寿).

OPPOSITE LEFT: A cap-sleeved *cheongsam* in nylon by Vivienne Tam, 2002. Several elements of this black dress are designed to evoke memories of the traditional *cheongsam*. For example, it is decorated with satin piping and floral embroidery. The lace trimming embellishing the side of the dress and the hem is reminiscent of the slip worn under *cheongsam* of the 1930s.

OPPOSITE RIGHT: A bias-cut *cheongsam*-inspired dress in silk and fur by British designer John Galliano for Christian Dior, fall 1997. The black shimmery dress has a mandarin collar that is decorated with petal-like motifs created by pearls. Fabric-wrapped buttons line the asymmetrical opening and the side of the *cheongsam*. It also has a high side slit that reveals the long legs of the wearer. The cuffs and hem of the dress are trimmed with fur.

children too. Unless you have a huge capital, you cannot survive in this business."[33] It was also extremely difficult to hire workers to help out in the shop. Both Master Lok and Master Ching recalled that by the 1980s, only Malaysian workers were available. However, it was rather expensive to hire them because the government's labour policy stated that for every Malaysian worker hired, four Singaporeans had to be hired.[34] As a result of shortage of workers, Master Lok only made *cheongsam* for his regular customers while Master Ching had to turn away his customers.

Singapore Fashion Designers and Their Interpretation of the *Cheongsam*

Western and Asian designers have always been inspired by the *cheongsam*. Since 1993, the traditional Chinese dress has appeared regularly on international fashion runways. The return of Hong Kong to China in 1997 created a resurgence of all styles Chinese throughout the West.[38] In the same year, British designer John Galliano designed an entire collection inspired by Shanghai and the *cheongsam*. Shanghai Tang, a more contemporary brand, marketed its brand of *cheongsam* as one made by the Chinese for an international clientele.[39] A new wave of Chinese and Chinese-American designers such as Vivienne Tam, Anna Sui, Hang Feng, Yeohlee and Shiatzy Chen, amongst others, have begun to draw on their own cultures as a source of inspiration for their collections.

Alongside the revival of the *cheongsam* in the West by fashion designers and the influence of highly successful recent Chinese films that featured women in *cheongsam* – *Center Stage* (1992), *In the Mood for Love* (2000), *Everlasting Regret* (2005) and *The Message* (2009), just to name a few – a group of local fashion designers including both established and up-and-coming ones, such as Allan Chai, Lai Chan, Tan Yoong, Tan Sheau Yun and Priscilla Shunmugam, amongst others, has been re-interpreting the *cheongsam* to suit the modern context. Some of these designers have been in the fashion industry for more than 20 years while others, such as Priscilla Shunmugam, have only just launched their labels. This group of producers was not formally trained in the making of traditional *cheongsam*, unlike

RIGHT: Fashion designer Vivienne Tam arriving at the 7th Annual National Arts Awards held in New York, 2002. She is wearing a *cheongsam* she designed.

OPPOSITE: A model walks the runway at the Vivienne Tam Fall 2006 fashion show at Bryant Park, New York. The dress has the essential characteristics of *cheongsam* such as the mandarin collar, asymmetrical opening, embroidery and piping.

the Shanghainese tailors of the early 20th century, although some have come into contact with them during their careers or have had Shanghainese tailors working as pattern drafters for them. Despite the lack of formal training, these producers of *cheongsam* share a similar vision – that is to design and make *cheongsam* a relevant dress option for the modern woman.

Even though the designers feel that the traditional *cheongsam* is beautiful and they have great respect for the Shanghainese tailors, they feel that the traditional cut does not suit the lifestyles and frames of women today. For example, Lai Chan has observed that women have longer torsos now and hence has added 1.5cm to the body of the *cheongsam* he makes.[40] He also straightened the cut in the hip area so that the fabric falls nicely. The traditional *cheongsam* tailoring has a rounded cut at the hips that he feels would cling and bulge especially when the woman is seated.[41] Priscilla Shunmugam created the *cheongsam* with a peplum – fabric attached to the waistline to create a hanging frill – that helped to conceal the lower abdomen of the wearer who was uncomfortable with the form-fitting cut of the traditional *cheongsam*. There are also other designers who incorporated the halter-neck design in their *cheongsam* in response to Singapore's tropical climate.

To make sure that the *cheongsam* they design is convenient and appropriate for the lifestyle of contemporary women, designers such as Tan Sheau Yun and Priscilla Shunmugam test-fit their own creations before launching them in their shops. They wear them to run errands and drive a car. According to Shunmugam, this process is important because her customers will only buy the *cheongsam* she designs if the garments suit their busy lifestyles and do not restrict their movement.

Despite the emergence of different versions of the modern *cheongsam*, most of the designers, if not all, retain one fundamental feature of the traditional *cheongsam*: the mandarin collar. Tan Yoong, who specialises in making bridal wear including custom-made *cheongsam*, insists that a modern *cheongsam* can have a different silhouette from the traditional cut as long as it still has a mandarin collar and a good fit.[42]

OPPOSITE LEFT: A silk *cheongsam* with gingham print, 2005. It has printed fabric-wrapped buttons on the asymmetrical opening and its side.

OPPOSITE RIGHT: Fuchsia *cheongsam* in wool and silk by John Galliano for Christian Dior's autumn 2009 ready-to-wear (RTW) collection. The dress has a stand-up collar and an asymmetrical opening made in a red floral panel decorated with small flowers while knotted buttons line the panel at regular intervals. The sash with tassels and the tight hem give the bubble-shaped dress a sharper silhouette.

FOLLOWING PAGES, LEFT TO RIGHT: A model wearing a gown with a high collar and cut-in sleeves by Taiwanese designer Shiatzy Chen, spring/summer 2012 RTW collection; Taiwanese celebrity Lin Zhiling wearing a back-revealing *cheongsam*-inspired dress by Shanghai Tang, 2011; a model wearing another creation inspired by the *cheongsam* by John Galliano for Christian Dior, fall 1997.

Conclusion

Although the *cheongsam* will probably never regain the popularity it had in the 1950s and 1960s, it is unlikely that the dress will completely disappear. Since the introduction of the *cheongsam* in China in the early 1920s, it has evolved continuously in its form and significance in response to the changing needs of its wearer. The longevity of the *cheongsam* would not have been possible without the help of the Shanghainese tailors who were not only valued for their workmanship but also their ability to adapt Western techniques into the making of the *cheongsam*. Even though most of them have retired from the scene, they have now been gradually replaced by a new group of producers who continue to interpret the *cheongsam* according to the needs of modern women. Today, the *cheongsam* continues to be part of the wardrobe of a small group of women in Singapore. It is still worn on special occasions such as weddings, banquets and on Chinese New Year. It continues to be the perennial formal wear for the wives of Singapore's political leaders and First Ladies. For the older women, the traditional dress is a reflection of their identity as a Chinese as well as respectable and elegant formal wear. On the other hand, younger professionals prefer the *cheongsam* that is convenient, suits their busy lifestyles and more importantly distinguishes them from other women. This type of *cheongsam* has a different silhouette from the traditional *cheongsam* while maintaining the characteristic mandarin collar. It is also likely to be more expensive because of its unusual design that allows it to stand out from the crowd. In short, younger women who wear the *cheongsam* now see it as a fashion commodity rather than a garment which expresses their Chinese identity and cultural heritage.[43]

OPPOSITE CLOCKWISE
FROM TOP LEFT: Detail of
embroidery on a silk
satin *cheongsam*; detail
of fan-shaped motif on a
Swiss cotton *cheongsam*;
detail of leave motif
on a silk *cheongsam*;
detail of floral burn-out
pattern on a silk crêpe
cheongsam.

Glossary

APPLIQUÉ

BATIK

BATIK

BURN-OUT PATTERN

Appliqué

The term is derived from the French verb *appliquer*, which means "to put on" or "to overlay", and refers to the application of decoration onto the surface of a fabric. This is usually achieved by cutting out fabric or lace designs and attaching them to another fabric or lace by means of embroidery or stitching. It is one of the methods used by Shanghainese tailors to embellish *cheongsam* meant for formal occasions. Trimmings, including cording created by twisting two or more yarns together, are also often used by tailors to decorate a plain fabric, such as silk satin.

Batik

In Singapore, *batik* was associated with pan-Malayan identity and nationalism in the 1960s. It is a resist-dyeing technique used to decorate finished fabrics which are then popularly used for making *sarong*, particularly in Indonesia, Malaysia and Singapore. *Batik* can be drawn by hand (*tulis*) or with the canting cap, a waxing stamp made of copper. Screen printing was incorporated into *batik* in the 1950s. *Batik* designs are diverse and deeply rooted in traditional agrarian philosophy. Some of the more popular styles are *garis miring* (diagonally running motifs), *nitik* (small dashes or dots), *ceplok* (motifs based on the five cardinal directions – north, south, east, west and centre), cross sections of fruits, and *semen* (stylised motifs inspired by nature). By the 1950s and 1960s, it was also used to make dresses, *kebaya* suits, men's shirts and *cheongsam*.

Burn-out pattern

A burn-out pattern is used to describe fabric such as brocade, velvet or lace that has a patterned effect produced by using yarns of two different fibres and destroying all or part of one of the yarns. A fabric with a burn-out pattern is known as devoré. A burn-out effect can be produced by using chemicals to dissolve

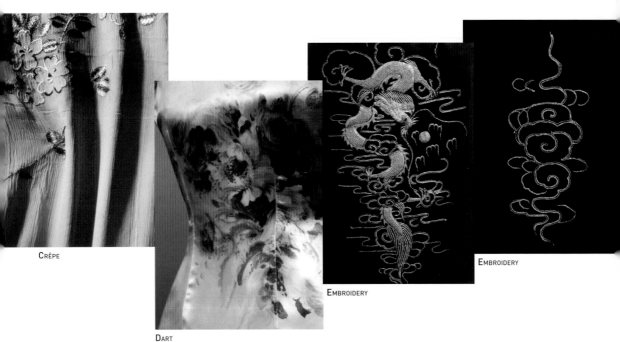

CRÊPE

DART

EMBROIDERY

EMBROIDERY

parts of the fabric to create the desired pattern. The technique originated in France in the early 20th century and became extremely popular in fashion design during the 1920s. In the 1930s, velvet with a burn-out floral pattern was often used to make *cheongsam*. Velvet is a fabric with short, closely woven pile created from extra lengthwise yarns. Usually the pile is cut to create a soft, rich texture and is thus suitable as a fabric for evening wear. The burn-out pattern dissolves part of the velvet, leaving sheer areas of the fabric. Therefore, the *cheongsam* has to be worn with a slip underneath.

Crêpe

Crêpe is a general term used for fabrics with an overall crinkled texture achieved by subjecting the yarn to a tight twist in opposite directions. It can be found in both silk and synthetic fibres. Examples of crêpe include chiffon and georgette although the latter is more textured than the former. Between 1931 and 1935, *cheongsam* made in crêpe was in vogue in China. It was lightweight and, more importantly, the sheerness of the fabric highlighted the figure of the wearer. This coincided with the larger social movement of female emancipation

in China, which was manifested in the liberalisation of women's dress. For example, the *cheongsam* became more form-fitting than it had been in the 1920s, and nude stockings, which showed off rather than concealed the skin of the wearer, were preferred.

Dart

Sewing term for V-shaped tuck used to make the garment conform to the body shape hence making it more three-dimensional. Used frequently at the shoulders, waist, or in the side seam under the arm. Darts first appeared in the West during the Gothic period but were introduced into the making of *cheongsam* only in the early 20th century by the *Hong Bang* (红帮) tailors who were well-versed in making Western garments. It was only in the 1950s that darts began to be used extensively at the bust and waist in *cheongsam* to make it more form-fitting, which transformed the previously flat and angular garment.

Embroidery

This refers to the technique of decorating fabric with fancy needlework or trimming using coloured cotton

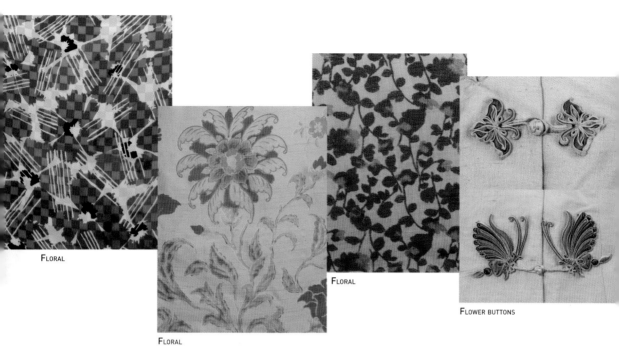

Floral

Floral

Floral

Flower buttons

thread and other types of materials such as silk or metallic threads, beads, pearls and sequins. One of the greatly admired skills of a Shanghainese tailor was the ability to create beautiful embroidery work by hand. Since the introduction of the *cheongsam* to Singapore in the 1920s, tailors have liked to embellish the garment with embroidered flowers. By the 1950s and 1960s, auspicious motifs such as dragons and phoenixes were embroidered onto the *cheongsam* using sequins, beads and metallic threads. These embroidered *cheongsam* not only looked glamorous and suitable for evening functions but were also greatly admired as intricate works of art.

Floral

The floral pattern, which evokes images of spring and romance, is one of the most popular fabric patterns found on Western frocks, *samfoo* and the *cheongsam* from the 1950s and 1960s. It was first mass-produced with the introduction of printing during the Industrial Revolution in the 19th century. There are several ways to arrange floral motifs. Flowers could be so closely packed together that the background almost disappears. An all-over non-directional design allows more than

half of the background to be covered in motifs. There is also the bouquet motif that allows the fabric to be filled with a variety of flowers or the same motif used repeatedly. The introduction of silk-screen printing in the late 1920s and early 1930s allowed floral motifs to be created with a watercolour effect on silk and cotton. In the 1930s, women wearing floral motif *cheongsam* were often depicted in calendar posters. By the 1950s and 1960s, the motif became even more widespread with the introduction of synthetic fabrics.

Flower buttons

Flower buttons (*hua niu*; 花钮) are the decorative buttons and loops which are stitched to fasten the collar and lapel of the *cheongsam*. The designs and compositions vary from plain to intricate. Traditional designs include floral, animal and insect motifs, and auspicious symbols such as the gourd and the Chinese character *shou* (寿), which symbolise fertility and longevity respectively. The flower buttons on the collar and the front flap are more intricately designed while those at the side of the slit are usually of a simpler pattern such as a knot. Most of the flower buttons found on *cheongsam* were designed to

GEOMETRIC PATTERN

GEOMETRIC PATTERN

FLOWER BUTTONS

GEOMETRIC PATTERN

complement the pattern of the fabric and sometimes were similar to the floral motifs found on the fabric. The fabric used to make these buttons is usually the same as the *cheongsam* fabric, cut on the bias (diagonally across the stitch of the cloth). It is then stiffened with starch made from flour and water or with a fine wire inserted in between the fabric before it is twisted and sewn together into the desired pattern. For more complicated designs, the buttons are stuffed with cotton to achieve the desired motif. Shanghainese tailors, especially those from Fuzhou, were known for their skills in making flower buttons by hand. Flower buttons were an integral part of the *cheongsam* design, especially in the 1930s and from the 1960s to the 1980s. *Cheongsam* with complex flower buttons were more expensive as they were all hand-made. The declining popularity of *cheongsam* together with the retirement of Singapore's Shanghainese tailors by the 1980s meant that tailors and fashion designers now had to source these custom-made buttons from China.

Geometric patterns

Fabrics with geometric patterns were popular for making *cheongsam* from the 1930s. Geometric patterns include circles, squares, triangles, cartouches, spirals, crescents, stars, pinwheels, polka dots and different types of plaid or tartan such as gingham. In the 1930s, geometric patterns reflecting Art Deco fashions were the trend. Art Deco motifs were known for their angular, zigzag and stepped forms, sweeping curves, chevron patterns, geometric patterns and bright solid colours. They first became popular in Europe in the 1920s. Geometric patterns became fashionable again in conjunction with the Optical Art movement of the 1960s. Optical Art motifs are made of spirals, circles and squares arranged geometrically to create an illusion of movement. They originated from the 1920s Optical Art movement, which experimented with optical perceptions and illusions. The introduction of synthetic fabrics in the 1950s and 1960s gave women the option of making *cheongsam* with fabrics printed or woven with exciting geometric and Optical Art motifs.

Piping

Piping refers to the narrow strip of fabric that may be inserted between two layers of fabric before stitching to create a decorative effect. It could be sewn to the

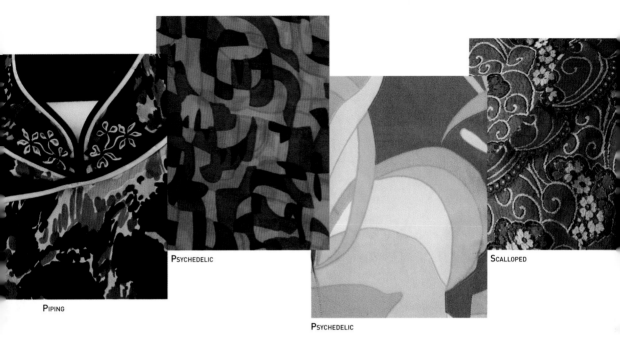

PSYCHEDELIC

SCALLOPED

PIPING

PSYCHEDELIC

seam of the collar, asymmetrical opening, cuff, sides of the slits and hem of the *cheongsam*. The fabric is usually cut on a bias, which is the diagonal direction of the fabric because it allows a greater stretch and better drape. The purpose of the piping is to embellish and accentuate the silhouette and curves of the wearer even from a distance. The colour of the piping could either match the background colour of the *cheongsam* fabric or a brighter shade found on the fabric. Piping is sometimes combined with binding, which refers to the strip of fabric inserted into the hem or seam of a *cheongsam*. Both binding and piping could be used together by creating two strips of different coloured fabric, a style which was popular in the 1930s. The two strips could be of the same width or one wider than the other. For the latter, the broader strip would be made of the same colour as the lining of the *cheongsam* while the narrower strip would most likely be of a brighter colour found on the fabric.

Psychedelic

Fabrics with psychedelic motifs are the opposite of geometric-patterned fabric. They are characterised by irregular patterns, swirling shapes and neon colours. They symbolised the youth movement that emerged after the Second World War and were popular during the hippy movement of the late 1960s. The term "psychedelic style" describes art that is created under the influence of hallucinogenic drugs. It also borrowed heavily from the Optical Art and Pop Art of the 1960s. French designer Yves Saint Laurent and Italian designer Emilio Pucci were known for their brightly coloured psychedelic prints of the 1960s. *Cheongsam* with psychedelic prints were popular in Singapore in the late 1960s and early 1970s because they gave the *cheongsam* a more updated and colourful look, in line with the youth movement of the same period.

Scalloped

Named after the shellfish, this refers to edges with a continuous line of regular, semi-circular curves. It was extremely popular as a form of decoration for the *cheongsam*. It could be used to decorate the collar of the Western-style jacket that goes with the *cheongsam*, the side of a 1930s slip worn under a crêpe *cheongsam* or the garment's cuffs or hem.

Endnotes

Introduction

1. This introduction is adapted from Lee Chor Lin, "Chinese Dress in Singapore", in Jasleen Dhamija (ed.), *Berg Encyclopedia of World Dress and Fashion, Volume 4: South Asia and Southeast Asia* (Oxford and New York: Berg Publishers, 2010), pp. 412–8.
2. R. H. Bruce Lockhart, *Return To Malaya* (London: Putnam, 1936), p. 116.

Chapter 1

1. Joanne Entwistle, *The Fashioned Body: Fashion, Dress and Modern Social Theory* (Cambridge, UK: Polity, 2000), pp. 48–9. According to Entwistle, fashion refers to a system of dress found in societies where social mobility is possible; it has its own particular relations of production and consumption, again found in a particular sort of society; and it is characterised by a logic of regular and systemic change.
2. Mark Ravinder Frost and Yu-Mei Balasingamchow, *Singapore: A Biography* (Singapore: Editions Didier Millet and the National Museum of Singapore, 2009), p. 340.
3. Chan Heng Chee, "Notes on the mobilization of women into the economy and politics of Singapore", *Commentary*, Vol. 5, No. 1 (October 1987), p. 61.

Mrs Robert Eu (daughter of self-made China-born merchant Chia Yee Soh) and Ms Amy Laycock (daughter of John Laycock, legislative councillor from 1948 to 1955) participated in the first City Council elections in 1948. In 1951, Mrs Vilasini Menon, a lawyer educated at Madras University, became the first and only woman to be elected in the Legislative Council. War heroine, social worker and school teacher Mrs Elizabeth Choy was appointed as a nominated member of the Legislative Council from 1951 to 1955 by the Governor of Singapore.

4. Vivienne Wee, "The Ups and Downs of Women's Status in Singapore: A Chronology of Some Landmark Events (1950–1970)", *Commentary*, Vol. 7, No. 2 & 3 (December 1987), p. 6.
5. Audrey Chin and Constance Singam, *Singapore Women Re-presented* (Singapore: Landmark Books, 2004), p. 143.
6. C. M. Turnbull, *A History of Singapore, 1819–1988* (Singapore: Oxford University Press, 1989), p. 285. Mdm Chan Choy Siong (wife of Minister Ong Pang Boon) was born to a poor family in Singapore in 1934 but was better educated than most of her female contemporaries. She organised mass rallies, set up a Women's Affairs

Bureau in 1959 and was pivotal in persuading the PAP to include "One Man, One Wife" as one of the elections campaign slogans the same year. She became a PAP city councillor in 1957 at the age of 23 and served on the party's central executive committee from 1957 to 1963. She also ran programmes for women and children and formed women's committees in PAP's branches. She retired from politics in 1970.

7. Ibid., p. 143. Mrs Seow Peck Leng was one of the founding members of SCW and an active social worker.
8. Wee, p. 7.
9. Ibid.
10. Turnbull, p. 281. Prior to this, Singapore was still largely dependent on international entrepôt commerce, servicing Malayan staple commodities and on income from British military bases. But in 1961, the government engaged the help of distinguished Dutch economist Dr Albert Winsemius to devise a four-year economic policy. Dr Winsemius had played a major role in Holland's economic revival after the Second World War.
11. Wee, p. 7
12. Chan, p. 65.
13. Turnbull, p. 249.
14. Ibid., p. 284.
15. Ibid., p. 314.
16. Frost and Balasingamchow, p. 337.

17. Chin and Singam, p. 133.
18. Entwistle, p. 10.
19. Ms Wong Moe Chng, born in 1914, came to Singapore and Penang to teach in 1935. She described the *cheongsam* as neat and presentable and a form of everyday dress for Shanghainese women like her. Oral History Centre, National Archives of Singapore, Accession No. 000300.
20. Valerie Steele, *Fifty Years of Fashion: New Look to Now* (New Haven: Yale University Press, 1998), p. 11. French couturier Christian Dior's 1947 "New Look" was defined by soft sloping shoulders, a full bust and a cinched-in waist above full, long skirts that captured the immediate attention of Carmel Snow, the editor of American fashion magazine *Harper's Bazaar* who commented, "Your dresses have such a new look."
21. Angela Partington, "Popular Fashion and Working Class Affluence", in J. Ash and E. Wilson (eds.), *Chic Thrills: A Fashion Reader* (London: Harper Collins, 1992), p. 157.
22. Joanne Finkelstein, *After a Fashion* (Carlton South, Vic., Australia: Melbourne University Press, 1996), p. 41.
23. Master Lok Chye Kwai was born in Shanghai in 1925. He came to Singapore in 1937 to learn tailoring. Oral history interview by Chung May Khuen, 6 June 2006.

24. Mrs Nancy Lim was born in 1936 in Singapore. She was the first female sales representative of Pearl and Dean Advertising (SEA) in Singapore in 1959. Oral history interview by Chung May Khuen, 22 August 2005.

25. Mrs Lau Siew Yee was from Segamat, Johor, Malaysia. She came to Singapore to work as a telegraph operator at Telecoms in 1948. In Malaysia, she wore the *samfoo* to work. However, she began to wear the *cheongsam* to the office in Singapore. Oral history interview by Chung May Khuen, 26 August 2005.

26. Chung Khiaw Bank was established in 1950 by the Aw family. It was known to be a bank that served both the rich and the masses. It was bought over by Slater Walker Securities in 1971 and then by another Singapore bank, United Overseas Bank, in the same year.

27. Ong Kiat Beng, "The cheongsam is playing a losing game in young fashion", *The Straits Times*, 19 January 1971, p. 20.

28. "Courteous and prompt service to all", *The Straits Times*, 24 July 1965, p. 12.

29. Elizabeth Tio Hui Tang, "More Than Just a Fashion Show: Women's Clothes and Chinese Identity in 1950 Singapore", unpublished dissertation (National University of Singapore, 2010), p. 41. *Saturday Review* was established in 1949 and it contained several segments that disseminated information, ideas and images of how women should dress and what their roles were in society.

30. Chiang Hai Ding, *A History of Straits Settlements Foreign Trade 1870–1915* (Singapore: National Museum of Singapore, 1978), p. 4. Ships were exempted from the payment of import and export duties, tonnage and port dues, wharfage and anchorage dues, port clearance fees and stamp duties.

31. Sachdev Durgadass was born in 1919, in Punjab, India. He set up his business in textile trading in Singapore in 1946. Oral History Centre, National Archives of Singapore, Accession No. 00153.

32. Mr Jaswant Singh Bajaj was born in 1935, in Punjab, India. His father set up the S. Pritam Singh Co. after the Second World War dealing with textiles. In 1953, Mr Bajaj joined his father's company. Oral History Centre, National Archives of Singapore, Accession No. 000167.

33. Susannah Handley, *Nylon the Manmade Fashion Revolution: A Celebration of Design from Art Silk to Nylon and Thinking Fibres* (London: Bloomsbury, 1999), p. 80.

34. Lurex was first mentioned in *The Straits Times* in 1957 as a fabric that has a new metallic yarn woven into it. It gives the fabric a glitter that sparkles, does not tarnish and could be washed without damage. "Good news for the Fair Sex, Glitter that won't wash off!", *The Straits Times*, 14 April 1957, p. 6.

35. Entwistle, p. 117.

36. Chua Beng Huat, *Life Is Not Complete Without Shopping: Consumption Culture in Singapore* (Singapore: Singapore University Press, 2003), p. 76.

37. Mr Sharul Said was born in 1969 in Singapore. He ventured into the art of *batik* at the age of 16. Oral history interview, 27–8 July 2005, by Kartini Saparudin for the National Museum of Singapore.

38. *Crafted in Malaysia* (Kuala Lumpur: Malaysian Handicraft Development Corporation, 2007), p. 35. Kelantan Silk or Songket is a luxurious gold brocade on silk fabric for the Malay *sarong* and *baju*. Gold or silver metallic threads are inserted between the warps to produce slightly embossed, intricate patterns above the background. The main production centres are the eastern states of Kelantan, Terengganu and Pahang in Malaysia.

39. Nylex is a durable strong nylon thread fabric imported from Japan into Singapore in the early 1960s.

40. Valerie Steele, *The Black Dress* (New York: Collins Design, 2007), p. 10.

41. For example, tips on how to look best during the Chinese New Year dressed in a black *cheongsam* with red motifs were featured in a newspaper in 1960, "The only way to brighten up the black cheongsam is to wear a pair of matching red earrings. And then with black gloves and black shoes. It's a winner." "Cheongsam Dos and Don'ts", *The Singapore Free Press*, 15 January 1960, p. 8.

42. Oral history interview by Chung May Khuen with Mrs Nancy Lim, 22 August 2005.

43. "Where have all those Slinkies Gone?", *Her World*, Vol. 9, No. 10 (October 1968), p. 33.

44. Oral history interview by Chung May Khuen with Mr Lok Chye Kwai, 6 June 2006.

45. Ong, p. 20.

Chapter 2

1. For an in-depth discussion of the changes in the everyday life of Singaporeans see Chua (1989; 1997, Chapter 8).

2. *Singapore: The Encyclopedia* (Singapore: Editions Didier Millet and the National Heritage Board, 2006), p. 120.

3. "Obituaries: Elizabeth Choy", *The Telegraph*, 10 October 2006. In 1950, she ran for elections as an independent candidate and although she failed to be elected, she was nominated as a member of the Legislative Council between 1951 and 1955. She spoke out for the poor and needy and campaigned for the development

of social services and family planning.

4. Zhou Mei, *Elizabeth Choy: More than a War Heroine* (Singapore: Landmark Books, 1995), p. 107. Mrs Choy was invited to speak about the aspirations of the people in Singapore and Malaya by the British Foreign Office in 1953 to the Canadians and Americans. She was selected because the Office felt that she was a convincing spokesperson and a goodwill ambassador.

5. Ibid., p. 94. Mrs Choy was first invited to meet Princess Elizabeth (now Queen Elizabeth II) in 1946 on behalf of the nurses who volunteered their services with the Medical Auxiliary Services during the Japanese invasion. She was dressed in a floral silk *cheongsam* and had a pink carnation in her hair.

6. Ibid. This *cheongsam* was custom-made at See Kwei Sung on Orchard Road, by a Shanghainese tailor for $130.

7. Ibid., p. 56.

8. *Singapore: The Encyclopedia*, p. 51. Mr Aw Boon Par was the younger son of Hakka herbalist Aw Chu Kin who established Eng Aun Tong in the 1870s in Rangoon, Burma. Aw Boon Par and his elder brother Aw Boon Haw succeeded their father's business after he passed away in 1908 and established Tiger Balm, which later became a household brand in Rangoon, Singapore, Malaysia, Hong Kong, China and the rest of Southeast Asia. In 1926, the brothers shifted their headquarters from Burma to Singapore.

9. Yap Joo Kim, *Far from Rangoon* (Singapore: Lee Teng Lay, 1994), p. 50. In the 1950s, under the leadership of Dato Lee, the bank expanded from two branches to ten in Singapore and Malaya.

10. Ibid., p. 56.

11. John and May Chu Harding, *Escape from Paradise* (Arizona: IDKPress, 2001), p. 20.

12. "Timeless elegance", *The Straits Times*, 19 January 1982, pp. 6–7. Eastern Paris Gown Shop was first established in Coleman Street, Singapore, in 1950. It charged $150 for a day-wear *cheongsam* with lining and an additional $30 for piping.

13. Oral history interview by Chung May Khuen, 24 October 2011.

14. Ms Edna Kung wrote "Chinese Fashion Notes" for *The Straits Times* between 1935 and 1936. In the column, she highlighted the latest fashion of the *cheongsam* and provided detailed descriptions of the dress.

15. Oral history interview by Chung May Khuen, 24 October 2011.

16. Ibid.

17. Bagan Siapiapi was once Indonesia's biggest fishing port. Almost 90 per cent of its community was Chinese, followed by the Malays and Batak.

18. Mdm Zhuo first saw the *cheongsam* being worn by her teacher, who came from Foochow, China. Subsequently, she arrived alone in Singapore in 1932 and pursued her higher education at Nanyang Girls' High School. She returned home and taught at her alma mater briefly before getting married in 1940. Oral history interview by Chung May Khuen, 6 July 2009.

19. Ibid.

20. Her parents were Mr and Mrs Lee Chong Miow. Mr Lee owned several properties including Lee and Fletcher Co., Singapore Photo Co. and Emporium Ltd. The family were members of the Seventh Day Adventist Church in Singapore.

21. She received an MBA in Finance from Cornell University, USA. Information provided by Mrs Jaya Mohideen, a close friend of Lee, to the National Museum of Singapore, 11 June 2009.

22. She liked swimming, bicycling, playing tennis and badminton. "Malayan Homes and Fashions", *The Straits Times*, 4 October 1949, p. 9.

23. She won a major award in a wildlife photography competition sponsored by the Indian government in 1959. In the same year, she also won a Silver Medal and was highly commended at the 10th Singapore International Salon. Sunny Giam, "Mrs Loke Goes Hunting Birds", *The Singapore Free Press*, 16 June 1959, p. 10.

24. *Birds in My Indian Garden* (1961), *Birds in the Sun* (1962) and *Treasure of Kenya* (1966). Information provided by Mrs Jaya Mohideen, 11 June 2009.

25. Wee Eng Hwa, *Cooking for the President* (Singapore: Wee Eng Hwa, 2010), p. 11. Mrs Wee's father, Mr Khor Chwee Thor, hailed from Hui An County, Fujian Province, China. He was a successful Hokkien entrepreneur who established a successful business building boats – lighters that plied the Singapore River to take goods to and from the warehouses along the river. He married a *nonya*, See Neo in 1914.

26. *Singapore: The Encyclopedia*, p. 587. Before Mr Wee became President of Singapore, he was a journalist and a diplomat.

27. Wee, p. 40.

28. Ibid., p. 28. Mr and Mrs Wee would dance to the music of live bands at leading hotels such as Raffles Hotel, Seaview Hotel and Adelphi Hotel.

Chapter 3

1. Hazel Clark, *The Cheongsam* (New York: Oxford University Press, 2000), p. 32.

2. Liu Yu, *Zhong Guo Qi Pao Wen Hua Shi* [The History of Chinese Qipao Culture] (Shanghai: Shanghai Renmin Meishu Chubanshe, 2011), p. 74.

3. Ibid., pp. 117–8. They were known thus because their business had become very prosperous by the early 20th century.
4. Oral history interview by Chung May Khuen with Master Lok Chye Kwai, 23 August 2006.
5. Oral History Centre, National Archives of Singapore, Accession No. 000326. Hou Sing was born on the outskirts of Shanghai, China, in 1911. He became an apprentice at the age of 12 and came to Singapore when he was 17.
6. Oral history interview by Chung May Khuen, 23 August 2006.
7. Oral History Centre, National Archives of Singapore, Accession No. 000325. Ching Foo Kun was born in Shanghai, China, in 1912. He became an apprentice from 1925 to 1930 and came to Singapore in 1936.
8. Oral History Centre, National Archives of Singapore, Accession No. 000326.
9. Ibid.
10. Oral History Centre, National Archives of Singapore, Accession No. 000444. This was attested to by both Mr Ching Foo Kun and Mr Ng Chee Seng, whose father came to Singapore to work as a tailor under the invitation of Mr Xu Jin Sheng in 1928. Mr Xu owned the shop Xu Jin Sheng Yang Huo Dian while Mr Ng's father opened the Hua Qiao Yang Fu Gong Si. Ng Chee Seng

was born in 1915 in Shanghai. He and his mother came to Singapore to join his father in 1929.
11. Oral history interview by Chung May Khuen, 23 August 2006.
12. Oral History Centre, National Archives of Singapore, Accession No. 000326.
13. Oral History Centre, National Archives of Singapore, Accession No. 000444.
14. Ibid.
15. Oral History Centre, National Archives of Singapore, Accession No. 000326. The samfoo comprises a blouse and trousers.
16. Ms Tan Sock Kern was born in Singapore in 1918. She became a teacher and subsequently the principal of Singapore Chinese Girls' School from 1952 to 1978. She started wearing the cheongsam in 1936/1937 when she was studying at Raffles College. Oral History Centre, National Archives of Singapore, Accession No. 001427.
17. For example, the ABC shop at Orchard Road before the Second World War had a branch shop for making cheongsam. However, when the business was wound up, the shop continued to refer customers who wanted to make cheongsam to the tailor. There was also the Chinese-owned Yue Tai Cheong Silk Shop and the Empress Fashion Company which had Shanghainese tailors who made cheongsam. Oral History

Centre, National Archives of Singapore, Accession No. 000326.
18. Oral history interview by Chung May Khuen, 23 August 2006.
19. Oral History Centre, National Archives of Singapore, Accession No. 000326.
20. Liu, p. 161.
21. Oral History Centre, National Archives of Singapore, Accession No. 000325.
22. Oral History Centre, National Archives of Singapore, Accession No. 000326.
23. Oral History Centre, National Archives of Singapore, Accession No. 000444.
24. Clark, p. 38.
25. Oral History Centre, National Archives of Singapore, Accession No. 000444.
26. Oral history interview by Chung May Khuen, 23 August 2006.
27. Ibid.
28. Oral History Centre, National Archives of Singapore, Accession No. 000326.
29. Oral history interview by Chung May Khuen, 23 August 2006.
30. Oral History Centre, National Archives of Singapore, Accession No. 000444.
31. Ibid.
32. Oral History Centre, National Archives of Singapore, Accession No. 000326.
33. Oral History Centre, National Archives of Singapore, Accession No. 000325. It cost about

S$2,000 a month to rent a shop front and S$100,000 to S$200,000 to start a tailor shop in 1983.
34. Oral history interview by Chung May Khuen, 23 August 2006.
35. Oral History Centre, National Archives of Singapore, Accession No. 001427.
36. Oral History Centre, National Archives of Singapore, Accession No. 000326.
37. Oral history interview by Chung May Khuen, 8 November 2010. Mdm Chen Hui Ying was born in Riau, Indonesia and came to Singapore with her parents when she was two or three years old. She started to wear a cheongsam when she became a teacher in 1957/1958.
38. Valerie Steele and John S. Major, China Chic: East Meets West (New Haven: Yale University Press, 1999), p. 69.
39. Wessie Ling, Fusionable Cheongsam (Hong Kong: Hong Kong Arts Centre, 2007), p. 27. Shanghai Tang was founded by Hong Kong businessman David Tang Wing Cheung in 1994.
40. Oral history interview by Chung May Khuen, 18 November 2011.
41. Adeline Chia, "Stitch of Genius", The Straits Times, 12 September 2011, Life section, p. C4.
42. Oral history interview by Chung May Khuen, 25 November 2011.
43. Oral history interview by Chung May Khuen, 18 November 2011.

Bibliography and Further Reading

"A man without pretensions", *The Straits Times*, 31 August 1985, p. 16.

Bian Xiangyang, "Origin of Qipao Fashion in Early Republic Period", *Journal of Donghua University* (English edition), Vol. 20, No. 4 (2003), pp. 21–26.

Chan Heng Chee, "Notes on the mobilization of women into the economy and politics of Singapore", *Commentary*, Vol. 5, No. 1 (October 1981), pp. 59–75.

"Cheongsam Dos and Don'ts", *The Singapore Free Press*, 15 January 1960, p. 8.

Chia, Adeline, "Stitch of Genius", *The Straits Times*, 12 September 2011, *Life* section, p. C4.

Chiang Hai Ding, *A History of Straits Settlements Foreign Trade 1870–1915* (Singapore: National Museum of Singapore, 1978)

Chin, Audrey, and Singam, Constance, *Singapore Women Re-presented* (Singapore: Landmark Books, 2004)

Chua Beng Huat, "The Business of Making a Living in Singapore", in Kernial Singh Sandhu and Paul Wheatley (eds.), *Management of Success: The Moulding of Modern Singapore* (Singapore: Institute of Southeast Asian Studies, 1989), pp. 1003–1021.

_____, *Political Legitimacy and Housing: Stakeholding in Singapore* (London: Routledge, 1997)

_____, *Life Is Not Complete Without Shopping: Consumption Culture in Singapore* (Singapore: Singapore University Press, 2003)

Clark, Hazel, *The* Cheongsam (New York: Oxford University Press, 2000)

Costumes Through Time: Singapore (Singapore: National Heritage Board and Fashion Designers Society, 1993)

"Courteous and prompt service to all", *The Straits Times*, 24 July 1965, p. 12.

Crafted in Malaysia (Kuala Lumpur: Malaysian Handicraft Development Corporation, 2007)

Dior, Christian, *Dior by Dior: the Autobiography of Christian Dior*, trans. Antonia Fraser (London: V&A Publications, 2007)

Entwistle, Joanne, *The Fashioned Body: Fashion, Dress and Modern Social Theory* (Cambridge, UK: Polity, 2000)

Fairservis, Walter A., *Costumes of the East* (Riverside, CT: The Chatham Press/The American Museum of Natural History, 1971)

Finkelstein, Joanne, *After a Fashion* (Carlton South, Vic., Australia: Melbourne University Press, 1996)

Finnane, Antonia, *Changing Clothes in China: Fashion, History, Nation* (New York: Columbia University Press, 2008)

Frost, Mark Ravinder, and Balasingamchow, Yu-Mei, *Singapore: A Biography* (Singapore: Editions Didier Millet and the National Museum of Singapore, 2009)

Garrett, Valery, *Chinese Dress: From the Qing Dynasty to the Present* (North Clarendon, VT: Tuttle Publishing, 2008)

Giam, Sunny, "Mrs Loke Goes Hunting Birds", *The Singapore Free Press*, 16 June 1959, p. 10.

"Good news for the Fair Sex, Glitter that won't wash off!", *The Straits Times*, 14 April 1957, p. 6.

Handley, Susannah, *Nylon the Manmade Fashion Revolution: A Celebration of Design from Art Silk to Nylon and Thinking Fibres* (London: Bloomsbury, 1999)

Harding, John, and Harding, May Chu, *Escape from Paradise* (Arizona: IDKPress, 2001)

Huang Qiang, *Yi Yi Bai Nian – Jin Bainian Zhongguo Fushi Fengshang zhi Bianqian* (Beijing: Wenhua Yishu Chubanshe, 2008)

Jackson, Beverley, *Shanghai Girl Gets All Dressed Up* (Berkeley, CA, and Toronto: Ten Speed Press, 2005)

Lam Wai Ning, "Fashion: Chinese ethnic clothing", unpublished academic exercise (Department of Sociology, National University of Singapore, 1991)

Lee Chor Lin, "Chinese Dress in Singapore", in Jasleen Dhamija (ed.), *Berg Encyclopedia of World Dress and Fashion, Volume 4: South Asia and Southeast Asia* (Oxford and New York: Berg Publishers, 2010)

Ling, Wessie, *Fusionable* Cheongsam (Hong Kong: Hong Kong Arts Centre, 2007)

Liu Yu, *Zhong Guo Qi Pao Wen Hua Shi* [*The History of Chinese* Qipao *Culture*] (Shanghai: Shanghai Renmin Meishu Chubanshe, 2011)

Lockhart, R. H. Bruce, *Return to Malaya* (London: Putnam, 1936)

"Malayan Homes and Fashions", *The Straits Times*, 4 October 1949, p. 9.

"Obituaries: Elizabeth Choy", *The Telegraph*, 10 October 2006.

Ong Kiat Beng, "The cheongsam is playing a losing game in young fashion", *The Straits Times*, 19 January 1971, p. 20.

Partington, Angela, "Popular Fashion and Working Class Affluence", in J. Ash and E. Wilson (eds.), *Chic Thrills: A Fashion Reader* (London: Harper Collins, 1992), pp. 145–61.

Roberts, Claire (ed.), *Evolution & Revolution: Chinese Dress, 1700s–1900s* (Sydney: Powerhouse Publishing and Museum of Applied Arts and Sciences, 1997)

Singapore: The Encyclopedia (Singapore: Editions Didier Millet and the National Heritage Board, 2006)

Steele, Valerie, *Fifty Years of Fashion: New Look to Now* (New Haven: Yale University Press, 1998)

_____, *The Black Dress* (New York: Collins Design, 2007)

_____, and Major, John S., *China Chic: East Meets West* (New Haven: Yale University Press, 1999)

The Evergreen Classic – Transformation of the Qipao, exhibition catalogue (Hong Kong: Hong Kong Museum of History, 2011)

"Timeless elegance", *The Straits Times*, 19 January 1982, pp. 6–7.

Tio Hui Tang, Elizabeth, "More Than Just a Fashion Show: Women's Clothes and Chinese Identity in 1950 Singapore", unpublished dissertation (National University of Singapore, 2010)

Turnbull, Constance Mary, *A History of Singapore, 1819–1988* (Singapore: Oxford University Press, 1989)

Wee, Vivienne, "The Ups and Downs of Women's Status in Singapore: A Chronology of Some Landmark Events (1950–1970)", *Commentary*, Vol. 7, No. 2 & 3 (December 1987), pp. 5–12.

Wee Eng Hwa, *Cooking for the President* (Singapore: Wee Eng Hwa, 2010)

"Where have all those Slinkies Gone?", *Her World*, Vol. 9, No. 10 (October 1968), pp. 32–33.

Wu Hao, *Du Hui Yun Chang: Xishuo Zhongguo Funü Fushi yu Shenti Geming, 1911–1935* (Hong Kong: San Lian Shu Dian, 2006)

Yap Joo Kim, *Far from Rangoon* (Singapore: Lee Teng Lay, 1994)

Zhou Mei, *Elizabeth Choy: More than a War Heroine* (Singapore: Landmark Books, 1995)

Index

Editor's note: *Italics* indicate photo references.

1911 Revolution 13

Ah Liew Ladies' Dress Maker *117*
Arab Street 53
Art Deco 150
Australia 100
Aw Boon Par 90
Aw Cheng Hu, Datin 90, *91–93*

baba 17, 22
Bagan Siapiapi 96
Bajaj, Jaswant Singh 53
baju Shanghai 10, 20
baju panjang 20
Bali *97*
Balsara, Dr Dadi 100
Bangkok 48
Basoeki Abdullah 100
Bata (shoe company) *47, 48*
batik 57, 58, *59, 61, 87, 111, 147*
Beijing 13
Ben Bang 114, *124*
Borneo 100
Bras Basah Road 28
Britannia, HMS *105*
British 17, *134*, 135
British Overseas Airways Corporation (BOAC) *46, 47*
Bukit Timah 119

Cantonese 17, 20, 22, 28, 124, 125
Cathay-Keris Film Productions 48
Chai, Allan 135
Chan Choy Siong 36, *38*
Chang, Eileen *see* Zhang Ailing
Chang, Grace *see* Ge Lan
Changi 86
changshan 13, 17, 22, 24
Chen, Shiatzy 135, *140, 145*
Chen Hui Ying 128
Cheng Jiao Ju *128*
Cheong Soo Pieng 100
Chiang Kai-shek 24
China 13, 14, 17, 96, 116, 123, 124, 135, 142, 148, 150
Chinese Civil War 119, 124
Chinese Ladies' Association *101*
Chinese Tailors' Union *119, 120–1*
Ching Foo Kun 119, 124, 130, 135
Chong, Mary Ann 74
Chotirmall 90

Choy, Mrs Elizabeth (Yong Su-Moi) 36, *76, 86, 87–89*
Choy Khun Heng 86
Chua Beng Huat, Professor 56, 79
Chung Khiaw Bank *46, 47*, 90
cinema 14
City Council 36
Convent of the Holy Infant Jesus (CHIJ) 86, *87*

Da Dong Restaurant *120–1*
deep-sea telephonic cables 14
Dior, Christian *134, 139, 141*
Durgadass, Sachdev 48, 53

East 62–63
Eastern Paris Gown Shop 90, *130*
Elizabeth II 86, *105, 107*
Eng Aun Tong 90
Eng Wah *48*
Entwistle, Joanne 35, 43
Eu, Mrs Robert 36, *38*
Europe 53, 82, 150

Finkelstein, Professor Joanne 44
France 148
Fuzhou 114, 150

Galliano, John *134*, 135, *139, 141*
Ge Lan (Grace Chang) 48
George VI 86, *120–1*
Girl Guides Association *105*
Goh Kok Kee, Mrs Constance 40
Gothic 148
Guangzhou 113, 114

Hainanese 17
Hakka 86, 124
Hang Feng 135
Her World 48, 104
High Street 28, 53, *65*, 90, 96, 119, 123
Ho Puay Choo 36
Hokkiens 125
Hollywood 100
Hong Bang Cai Feng (Feng Bang Cai Feng) 114, 148
Hong Kong 43, *47*, 48, 96, *99, 105*, 119, 123, 124, 135
Hou Sing 114, 116, 119, 123, 124, 125, 126, 130
Hunan *101*
Hwa Chiau Chinese and English School 104
Hyatt Hotel *90*

Industrial Revolution 149
Italy 70

Japan 53, 104, *105*
Japanese Occupation 86
Johor, Sultan of *105*

Kallang Park *90*
Kelantan Silk (Songket) *57*, 58
Kempetai (Japanese military police) 86
Kent, Duchess of *105*
Keong Saik Road 22
kerosang 22
Kho, Silvia *68–69*
Kim Way Local Products Company 96
King Edward VII College of Medicine 22
Koh Sok Hiong (Mrs Wee Kim Wee) 77, *83*, 104, 106, *107–8*
Koh Tin Kok 96
Kong Ngee 48
Korea 53, 104
Kuala Lumpur 94
Kudat, North Borneo 86
Kung, Edna 94

Labour Party 36
Lai Chan 135, 138
Lau Siew Yee, Mrs 46, 56, 58
Laycock, Amy 36
Le Di 48
Lee Chee San, Dato 90
Lee Choon Guan 22
Lee Hui Wong, Christina 100, *101–3, 127*
Lee Kuan Yew *78, 83*
Lee Kuan Yew, Mrs *78*, 79, *83, 84, 85*
Legislative Assembly 36
Legislative Council 36
Leong, Rosalind 46
Liangyou (*The Companion Pictorial*) 24
Lim, Catherine 79
Lim, Mrs Irene 94, *95*
Lim, Mrs Nancy 46, 56, 58, *69, 70, 71, 74, 110, 123, 128*
Lim Kim Lian, Veronica 68
Lin Dai (Linda) 48
Lin Huiyin 24
Lin Zhiling *140–1*
Ling Fang Intermediate Tailoring and Sewing School *128*
Liu Bao Jin 114
Lockhart, R. H. Bruce 28

Lok Chye Kwai 44, 74, 114, 116, 119, 123, 124, 125, 126, 135
Loke Wan Tho, Dato *83*, 100, *127*
Loke Yew, Mrs *100*
London 14, 70
Lu Xun 24

McQueen, Alexander *144*
magazines 14
Majeed (shop) 90
Malaysia 86, 94, 104, 135, 147
Manchu 13
May Fourth Movement 14, *21*
Menon, Vilasini 36
Metro (departmental store) 90
Modern Silk Store 90
Muslim Missionary Society Singapore (Jamiyah) *105*
Myanmar (Burma) 90

National Museum of Singapore 100
National University of Singapore (NUS) 56, 79
Nanyang Girls' High School 104
New York 70
newspapers 14
Ng Chee Seng 119, 123, 125, 130
Ngee Ann Girls' School 44
Ningbo 114
nonya 20, 22, 104, 123
North Bridge Road 28

Oh Siew Chen 36
Ong Teng Cheong *83*
Ong Teng Cheong, Mrs *83*
Optical Art *41*, 56, *60*, 150, 151
Orchard Road 119
Order of the British Empire (OBE) 86, *120–1*

P. Ramlee 58
Paris 14, 70
Partington, Dr Angela 44
Pasir Panjang 104
Peking University 13
Penang *97, 105*
People's Action Party (PAP) 36, 38
Peranakan 17, 20, 22, 94, 104
Philip, Prince *105*
Pop Art *41*, 56, 151
Progressive Party 36
Pucci, Emilio 151

Qing (Ching) dynasty 79, 80
qipao 24, 28, 126

Picture Credits

Radio Singapore *87*
Raffles College 28, *40*
Raffles Girls' School 94
Raffles Hotel *101*
Raft, George *100*
Rajaratnam, S. *87*
Ramos, Mrs Amelita M. *83*
Ramos, Fidel V. *83*
Rangoon 90

SABENA 46, *60*
St Andrew's School *87*
St Gregory's Place 90
Saint Laurent, Yves 151
sam 128
samfoo 46, 123, 149
San Yi Film 96
sari 58
sarong kebaya 20, 22, *23*, 58,
   68, 106
Saturday Review 48
Screen Voice 48
Second World War 35, 36, 43,
   96, 123, 128, 130, 151
selandang 96
Seow Peck Leng, Mrs 36
Shahrul Said 58
Shanghai 13, 14, 22, 24, 43,
   113, 114, 119, 130
Shanghai Nü Fu Xue Xi Suo 128
Shanghai Tang 135, *140–1*
Shanghainese 20, 28, 44, *99*,
   124, 125, 128, 130, 138, 142,
   147, 149, 150
Shangri-La Hotel 100
Shaw, George Bernard 24
Shaw Brothers 48
Sheares, Mrs Benjamin 80, *81*,
   83, *109*
Shunmugam, Priscilla *112*,
   135, 138, *142*
Sin Yik Embroiderers *117*
Singapore 14, 17, 20, 24, 35, 48,
   56, 80, 82, 90, 96, 100, 104,
   106, 113, 116, 119, 123, 124,
   130, 142, 147, 149, 150, 151
Singapore Constitution
   Exposition *69*
Singapore Council of Women
   (SCW) 36
Singapore Family Planning
   Association (SFPA) 40
Singapore General Hospital *87*
Singapore Polytechnic *69*
Singapore Tailors' Union *114*
Sino-Japanese War 119
Song Ong Siang 22
Songket *see* Kelantan Silk
Soong Mei-ling 24

steamship 14
Sui, Anna 135
Sumatra 96
Suzhou 114
synthetics *41*, 53, 56, 65, 94,
   122, 150

Tagore, Rabindranath 24
Tam, Vivienne *129*, *134*, 135,
   136, *137*
Tan Keong Saik 22
Tan Sheau Yun *111*, 135, 138
Tan Sock Kern 123, 128
Tan Teck Neo 22
Tan Yoong 135, 138, *143*
Teochews 125
The Companion Pictorial see
   Liangyou
The Happiness Journal 62–63
The Straits Times 48, 65, 94
Tianjin 13
Toh, Sylvia 104
Tokyo *106*
towkay 14

United States of America 53,
   100
University of the West of
   England 44

Victoria Memorial Hall *90*
Vogue 100

Wee Kim Wee *83*, 104
Wee Kim Wee, Mrs *see* Koh
   Sok Hiong
Women's Charter Bill (1961) 38
Wong, Suzie 80
Woodbridge Hospital 86
Wu Chuen Chuen *34*, *37*, *54–55*,
   71, *74*
Wu Liang Cai *120–1*

Xu Jin Sheng 119
Xu Zhimo 24

Yangzhou 114
Yeohlee 135
Yong Su-Moi *see* Choy,
   Elizabeth
York Hotel *105*
Yue Tai Cheong Silk Shop 27,
   29, *116*, *117*
Yusof Ishak *78*

Zhang Ailing (Chang, Eileen) 24
Zhejiang 114
Zhou Ling Fang *128*
Zhuo Yu Chun 96, *97–9*

Acknowledgements

This book would not have been possible without the efforts and expertise of many individuals. In writing this book, I have had the pleasure of meeting these wonderful ladies Mrs Nancy Lim, Mdm Zhuo Yu Chun, Mrs Irene Lim, Mdm Low Suet Hing, Mdm Chen Hui Ying, Mrs Lau Siew Yee, Mdm Chan Siok Fun who shared their experiences and knowledge of the significance of wearing the *cheongsam*. I am particularly grateful to the late Master Tailor Mr Lok Chye Kwai who not only gave his time but also shared his expertise on the subject which contributed to my understanding of the *cheongsam* on many levels. Special thanks to Goh Lai Chan, Tan Yoong, Tan Sheau Yun and Priscilla Shunmugan for sharing their thoughts on their interpretation of the *cheongsam*.

Immense thanks to the individuals and insititutions that have contributed to the *cheongsam* collection and photographs in this book. They are Datin Patricia Lim, Mrs Anita Benson, Mrs Betty Chen, the Hoe family, Mr and Mrs Melvin Poh, Jeffrey Teo, Veronica Lim Kim Lian, Chin May Nah, Goh Eck Kheng, the Wee family, Constance Sheares, Ms Angie Ng Chee Sun, Mrs Sylvia Kho, Mdm Tan Kim Lwi Agnes, Chong Sun Wah, Mr Jack Lee, Mdm Lim Siew Yong, Mrs Low Cheng Gim, Mr Lee Kuan Yew, Wu Sijing and Mrs Elizabeth Choy.

I am very grateful to Peter Lee, Mrs Jaya Mohideen, Mdm Chua Liang and Lionnel Lim who introduced many of these ladies who eventually donated their beautiful *cheongsam* to the Museum. Alex Soo from Method Imaging for his superb photography and Chan Xian Li for helping in the set up and production; Joanne Ng for assisting in the styling of the dresses during the shoot.

The individuals and institutions that have contributed photographs and granted permission to reproduced photographs have been gratefully acknowledged below.

Sincere thanks to colleagues at the National Heritage Board for their support and professionalism: colleagues from the Heritage Conservation Centre – Director Loh Heng Noi, Darren Wong, Adeline Chen, Johnny Chen, Karen Yap for retrieving the artefacts; Chuance Chen, Siti Suhailah Salim, Loh Boon Nee, Miki Komatsu, Elsie L. C. Wong for providing conservation support which enabled the photography of the *cheongsam* to proceed smoothly and on schedule. Gayathri Gill from the National Archives for attending to various requests and facilitating the use of photographs.

Special thanks also to colleagues at the National Museum of Singapore. Director Lee Chor Lin for her encouragement, guidance and advice. Chloe Ang for her curatorial support and managing the different parties involved in this book, Ong Chiew Yen for enabling the book to be completed within budget. The book also benefited significantly from the research help of Jessica Yeo, Joanna Toh Sok Chuan, Wang Meizhen, Gayne Lim Mei Fu and Simon Tong as well as compilation of oral histories.

Last but not least, I would like to express my appreciation to the team at Editions Didier Millet. Douglas Amrine and James Lui for their commitment, efficiency and meticulous editing, and Louise Brody's patience, endless energy and creativity that have been critical in seeing the book to completion.

Chung May Khuen